John Ruskin

Our Fathers Have Told us

Sketches of the History of Christendom. Third Edition

John Ruskin

Our Fathers Have Told us
Sketches of the History of Christendom. Third Edition

ISBN/EAN: 9783337030728

Printed in Europe, USA, Canada, Australia, Japan

Cover: Foto ©Lupo / pixelio.de

More available books at **www.hansebooks.com**

"OUR FATHERS HAVE TOLD US."

THE BIBLE OF AMIENS.

"OUR FATHERS HAVE TOLD US"

SKETCHES OF THE HISTORY OF CHRISTENDOM
FOR BOYS AND GIRLS WHO HAVE BEEN
HELD AT ITS FONTS

BY

JOHN RUSKIN, LL.D., D.C.L.

HONORARY STUDENT OF CHRIST CHURCH, OXFORD; AND
HONORARY FELLOW OF CORPUS CHRISTI
COLLEGE, OXFORD

THE BIBLE OF AMIENS

THIRD EDITION

GEORGE ALLEN, SUNNYSIDE, ORPINGTON

AND

156, CHARING CROSS ROAD, LONDON

1897

Printed by BALLANTYNE, HANSON & Co
At the Ballantyne Press

ST MARY.

By Cimabue at Assisi

EDITOR'S NOTE TO THE 1897 EDITION.

In this edition, Chapter I. has, for convenience of reference in the Index, been divided into numbered sections, and the references are throughout to the section of each chapter, and not to the page. Otherwise the text is unaltered, save for the correction of misprints in earlier editions, and one or two notes (marked Ed. 1897) added by the compiler of Appendix I., the two lists in Appendix II., and the Index.

PREFACE.

1. THE long abandoned purpose, of which the following pages begin some attempt at fulfilment, has been resumed at the request of a young English governess, that I would write some pieces of history which her pupils could gather some good out of;—the fruit of historical documents placed by modern educational systems at her disposal, being to them labour only, and sorrow.

What else may be said for the book, if it ever become one, it must say for itself: preface, more than this, I do not care to write: and the less, because some passages of British history, at this hour under record, call for instant, though brief, comment.

I am told that the Queen's Guards have gone to Ireland; playing "God save the Queen." And being, (as I have declared myself in the course of some letters to which public attention has been lately more than enough directed,) to the best of my knowledge, the staunchest Conservative in England, I am disposed gravely to question the propriety of the mission of the Queen's Guards on the employment commanded them. My own Conservative notion of the function of the Guards is that they should guard the Queen's throne and life, when threatened either by domestic or foreign enemy: but not that they should become a substitute for her inefficient police force, in the execution of her domiciliary laws.

2. And still less so, if the domiciliary laws which they are sent to execute, playing "God save the Queen," be perchance precisely contrary to that God the Saviour's law; and therefore, such as, in the long run, no quantity either of Queens, or Queen's men, *could* execute. Which is a question I have for these ten years been endeavouring to get the British public to consider—vainly enough hitherto; and will not at present add to my own many words on the matter. But a book has just been published by a British officer, who, if he had not been otherwise and more actively employed, could not only have written all my

books about landscape and picture, but is very singularly also of one mind with me, (God knows of how few Englishmen I can now say so,) on matters regarding the Queen's safety, and the Nation's honour. Of whose book ("Far out: Rovings retold"), since various passages will be given in my subsequent terminal notes, I will content myself with quoting for the end of my Preface, the memorable words which Colonel Butler himself quotes, as spoken to the British Parliament by its last Conservative leader, a British officer who had also served with honour and success.

3. The Duke of Wellington said: "It is already well known to your Lordships that of the troops which our gracious Sovereign did me the honour to entrust to my command at various periods during the war—a war undertaken for the express purpose of securing the happy institutions and independence of the country—at least one half were Roman Catholics. My Lords, when I call your recollection to this fact I am sure all further eulogy is unnecessary. Your Lordships are well aware for what length of period and

under what difficult circumstances they maintained the Empire buoyant upon the flood which overwhelmed the thrones and wrecked the institutions of every other people;—how they kept alive the only spark of freedom which was left unextinguished in Europe. . . . My Lords, it is mainly to the Irish Catholics that we all owe our proud predominance in our military career, and that I personally am indebted for the laurels with which you have been pleased to decorate my brow. . . . We must confess, my Lords, that without Catholic blood and Catholic valour no victory could ever have been obtained, and the first military talents might have been exerted in vain."

4. Let these noble words of tender Justice be the first example to my young readers of what all History ought to be. It has been told them, in the Laws of Fésole, that all great Art is Praise. So is all faithful History, and all high Philosophy. For these three, Art, History, and Philosophy, are each but one part of the Heavenly Wisdom, which sees not as man seeth, but with Eternal Charity; and because she rejoices not in Iniquity, *therefore* rejoices in the Truth.

For true knowledge is of Virtues only: of poisons and vices, it is Hecate who teaches, not Athena. And of all wisdom, chiefly the Politician's must consist in this divine Prudence; it is not, indeed, always necessary for men to know the virtues of their friends, or their masters; since the friend will still manifest, and the master use. But woe to the Nation which is too cruel to cherish the virtue of its subjects, and too cowardly to recognize that of its enemies!

CONTENTS.

	PAGE
PREFACE	vii

CHAPTER I

BY THE RIVERS OF WATERS 1

CHAPTER II.

UNDER THE DRACHENFELS . . . 51

CHAPTER III.

THE LION TAMER . . . 109

CHAPTER IV.

INTERPRETATIONS   164

APPENDIX I

CHRONOLOGICAL LIST OF PRINCIPAL EVENTS REFERRED TO IN THE 'BIBLE OF AMIENS' . . 259

APPENDIX II.

	PAGE
REFERENCES EXPLANATORY OF PHOTOGRAPHS TO CHAPTER IV.	263

APPENDIX III.

GENERAL PLAN OF 'OUR FATHERS HAVE TOLD US'	275
INDEX	279

ILLUSTRATIONS.

ST. MARY . . . . *Frontispiece*

PLATE I.—THE DYNASTIES OF FRANCE . *On p.* 15

PLATE II.—THE BIBLE OF AMIENS, NORTHERN
        PORCH BEFORE RESTORATION *To face p.* 51

PLATE III.—AMIENS, JOUR DES TRÉPASSÉS, 1880. ,, 109

        PLAN OF THE WEST PORCHES *On p.* 257

THE BIBLE OF AMIENS.

CHAPTER I.

BY THE RIVERS OF WATERS.

1. THE intelligent English traveller, in this fortunate age for him, is aware that, half-way between Boulogne and Paris, there is a complex railway-station, into which his train, in its relaxing speed, rolls him with many more than the average number of bangs and bumps prepared, in the access of every important French *gare*, to startle the drowsy or distrait passenger into a sense of his situation.

He probably also remembers that at this halting-place in mid-journey there is a well-served buffet, at which he has the privilege of "Dix minutes d'arrêt."

He is not, however, always so distinctly conscious that these ten minutes of arrest are granted to him within not so many minutes' walk of the central square of a city which was once the Venice of France.

2. Putting the lagoon islands out of question, the French River-Queen was nearly as large in compass as Venice herself; and divided, not by slow currents of ebbing and returning tide, but by eleven beautiful trout streams, of which some four or five are as large, each separately, as our Surrey Wandle, or as Isaac Walton's Dove; and which, branching out of one strong current above the city, and uniting again after they have eddied through its streets, are bordered, as they flow down, (fordless except where the two Edwards rode them, the day before Crecy,) to the sands of St. Valery, by groves of aspen, and glades of poplar, whose grace and gladness seem to spring in every stately avenue instinct with the image of the just man's life,—" Erit tanquam lignum quod plantatum est secus decursus aquarum."

But the Venice of Picardy owed her name, not to the beauty of her streams merely, but to their burden. She was a worker, like the Adriatic princess, in gold and glass, in stone, wood, and ivory; she was skilled like an

Egyptian in the weaving of fine linen; dainty as the maids of Judah in divers colours of needlework. And of these, the fruits of her hands, praising her in her own gates, she sent also portions to stranger nations, and her fame went out into all lands

"Un règlement de l'échevinage, du 12me avril 1566, fait voir qu'on fabriquait à cette epoque des velours de toutes couleurs pour meubles, des colombettes à grands et petits carreaux, des burailles croises, qu'on expédiait en Allemagne —en Espagne, en Turquie, et en Barbarie!"[1]

All-coloured velvets, pearl-iridescent colombettes! (I wonder what they may be?) and sent to vie with the variegated carpet of the Turk, and glow upon the arabesque towers of Barbary![2] Was not this a phase of provincial Picard life which an intelligent English traveller might do well to inquire into? Why should this fountain of rainbows leap up suddenly here by Somme; and a little Frankish maid write herself the sister of Venice, and the servant of Carthage and of Tyre?

[1] M. H. Dusevel, Histoire de la Ville d'Amiens. Amiens, Caron et Lambert, 1848; p. 305.
[2] Carpaccio trusts for the chief splendour of any festa in cities to the patterns of the draperies hung out of windows.

3. And if she, why not others also of our northern villages? Has the intelligent traveller discerned anything, in the country, or in its shores, on his way from the gate of Calais to the *gare* of Amiens, of special advantage for artistic design, or for commercial enterprise? He has seen league after league of sandy dunès. We also, we, have our sands by Severn, by Lune, by Solway. He has seen extensive plains of useful and not unfragrant peat,—an article sufficiently accessible also to our Scotch and Irish industries. He has seen many a broad down and jutting cliff of purest chalk; but, opposite, the perfide Albion gleams no whit less blanche beyond the blue. Pure waters he has seen, issuing out of the snowy rock; but are ours less bright at Croydon, at Guildford, or at Winchester? And yet one never heard of treasures sent from Solway sands to African; nor that the builders at Romsey could give lessons in colour to the builders at Granada? What can it be, in the air or the earth—in her stars or in her sunlight—that fires the heart and quickens the eyes of the little white-capped Amienoise soubrette, till she can match herself against Penelope?

4. The intelligent English traveller has of course no time to waste on any of these questions. But if he has bought his ham-sandwich, and is ready for the "En voiture, messieurs," he may perhaps condescend for an instant to hear what a lounger about the place, neither wasteful of his time, nor sparing of it, can suggest as worth looking at, when his train glides out of the station.

He will see first, and doubtless with the respectful admiration which an Englishman is bound to bestow upon such objects, the coal-sheds and carriage-sheds of the station itself, extending in their ashy and oily splendours for about a quarter of a mile out of the town; and then, just as the train gets into speed, under a large chimney tower, which he cannot see to nearly the top of, but will feel overcast by the shadow of its smoke, he *may* see, if he will trust his intelligent head out of the window, and look back, fifty or fifty-one (I am not sure of my count to a unit) similar chimneys, all similarly smoking, all with similar works attached, oblongs of brown brick wall, with portholes numberless of black square window. But in the midst of these fifty tall things that smoke, he will see one, a little taller than any, and more delicate, that does not smoke; and in the midst of these fifty masses of blank wall, enclosing 'works'—and doubtless producing works profitable and honourable to France and the world—he will see *one* mass of wall—not blank, but strangely wrought by the hands of foolish men of long ago, for the purpose of enclosing or producing no manner of profitable work whatsoever, but one—

"This is the work of God; that ye should believe on Him whom He hath sent"!

5. Leaving the intelligent traveller now to fulfil his vow of pilgrimage to Paris,—or wherever else God may be sending him,—I will suppose that an intelligent Eton boy or two, or thoughtful English girl, may care quietly to walk with me as far as this same spot of commanding view, and to consider what the workless—shall we say also worthless?—building, and its unshadowed minaret, may perhaps farther mean.

Minaret I have called it, for want of better English word. Flèche—arrow—is its proper name; vanishing into the air you know not where, by the mere fineness of it. Flameless—motionless—hurtless—the fine arrow; unplumed, unpoisoned, and unbarbed; aimless—shall we say also, readers young and old, travelling or abiding? It, and the walls it rises from — what have they once meant? What meaning have they left in them yet, for you, or for the people that live round them, and never look up as they pass by?

Suppose we set ourselves first to learn how they came there.

6. At the birth of Christ, all this hillside, and the brightly-watered plain below, with the corn-yellow champaign above, were inhabited by a Druid-taught race, wild enough in thoughts and ways, but under Roman government, and gradually becoming accustomed to hear the names, and partly to confess the power, of Roman gods. For three hundred years after the birth of Christ they heard the name of no other God.

Three hundred years! and neither apostles nor inheritors of apostleship had yet gone into all the world and preached the gospel to every creature. Here, on their peaty ground, the wild people, still trusting in Pomona for apples, in Silvanus for acorns, in Ceres for bread, and in Proserpina for rest, hoped but the season's blessing from the Gods of Harvest, and feared no eternal anger from the Queen of Death.

But at last, three hundred years being past and gone, in the year of Christ 301, there came to this hillside of Amiens, on the sixth day of the Ides of October, the Messenger of a new Life.

7. His name, Firminius (I suppose) in Latin, Firmin in French,—so to be remembered here in Picardy. Firmin, not Firminius; as Denis, not Dionysius; coming out of space—no one tells what part of space. But received by the pagan Amienois with surprised welcome, and seen of them—Forty days—many days, we may read—preaching acceptably, and binding with baptismal vows even persons in good society: and that in such numbers, that at last he is accused to the Roman governor, by the priests of Jupiter and Mercury, as one turning the world upside-down. And in the last day of the Forty—or of the indefinite many meant by Forty—he is beheaded, as martyrs ought to be, and his ministrations in a mortal body ended.

The old, old story, you say? Be it so; you will the more easily remember it. The Amienois remembered it so carefully, that, twelve hundred years afterwards, in the sixteenth century, they thought good to carve and paint the four stone pictures, Nos, 1, 2, 3, and 4 of our first choir photograph.* Scene 1st, St. Firmin arriving; scene 2nd, St. Firmin preaching; scene 3rd, St. Firmin baptizing; and scene 4th, St. Firmin beheaded, by an executioner with very red legs, and an attendant dog of the character of the dog in 'Faust,' of whom we may have more to say presently.

8. Following in the meantime the tale of St. Firmin, as of old time known, his body was received, and buried, by a Roman senator, his disciple (a kind of Joseph of Arimathea to St. Firmin), in the Roman senator's own garden. Who also built a little oratory over his grave. The Roman senator's son built a church to replace the oratory, dedicated it to Our Lady of Martyrs, and established it as an episcopal seat—the first of the French nation's. A very notable spot for the French nation, surely? One deserving, perhaps, some little memory or

---

* See *post*, App. ii., p. 266, note.—ED. (1897).

monument,—cross, tablet, or the like? Where, therefore, do you suppose this first cathedral of French Christianity stood, and with what monument has it been honoured?

It stood where we now stand, companion mine, whoever you may be; and the monument wherewith it has been honoured is this—chimney, whose gonfalon of smoke overshadows us—the latest effort of modern art in Amiens, the chimney of St. Acheul.

The first cathedral, you observe, of the *French* nation; more accurately, the first germ of cathedral *for* the French nation—who are not yet here; only this grave of a martyr is here, and this church of Our Lady of Martyrs, abiding on the hillside, till the Roman power pass away.

Falling together with it, and trampled down by savage tribes, alike the city and the shrine; the grave forgotten,—when at last the Franks themselves pour from the north, and the utmost wave of them, lapping along these downs of Somme, is *here* stayed, and the Frankish standard planted, and the French kingdom throned.

9. Here their first capital, here the first

footsteps[3] of the Frank in his France! Think of it. All over the south are Gauls, Burgundians, Bretons, heavier-hearted nations of sullen mind:—at their outmost brim and border, here at last are the Franks, the source of all Franchise, for this our Europe. You have heard the word in England, before now, but English word for it is none! *Honesty* we have of our own; but *Frankness* we must learn of these: nay, all the western nations of us are in a few centuries more to be known by this name of Frank. Franks, of Paris that is to be, in time to come; but French of Paris is in year of grace 500 an unknown tongue in Paris, as much as in Stratford-att-ye-Bowe. French of Amiens is the kingly and courtly form of Christian speech, Paris lying yet in Lutetian clay, to develope into tile-field, perhaps, in due time. Here, by soft-glittering Somme, reign Clovis and his Clotilde.

And by St. Firmin's grave speaks now another gentle evangelist, and the first Frank king's prayer to the King of kings is made

[3] The first fixed and set-down footsteps; wandering tribes called of Franks, had overswept the country, and recoiled, again and again. But *this* invasion of the so-called Salian Franks, never retreats again.

to Him, known only as "the God of Clotilde."

10. I must task the reader's patience now with a date or two, and stern facts—two—three—or more.

Clodion, the leader of the first Franks who reach irrevocably beyond the Rhine, fights his way through desultory Roman cohorts as far as Amiens, and takes it, in 445.[4]

Two years afterwards, at his death, the scarcely asserted throne is seized—perhaps inevitably — by the tutor of his children, Merovée, whose dynasty is founded on the defeat of Attila at Chalons.

He died in 457. His son Childeric, giving himself up to the love of women, and scorned by the Frank soldiery, is driven into exile, the Franks choosing rather to live under the law of Rome than under a base chief of their own. He receives asylum at the court of the king of Thuringia, and abides there. His chief officer in Amiens, at his departure, breaks a ring in two, and, giving him the half of it, tells him, when the other half is sent, to return.

---

[4] See note at end of chapter, as also for the allusions in p. 17, to the battle of Soissons.

And, after many days, the half of the broken ring is sent, and he returns, and is accepted king by his Franks.

The Thuringian queen follows him, (I cannot find if her husband is first dead—still less, if dead, how dying,) and offers herself to him for his wife.

"I have known thy usefulness, and that thou art very strong; and I have come to live with thee. Had I known, in parts beyond sea, any one more useful than thou, I should have sought to live with *him*."

He took her for his wife, and their son is Clovis.

11. A wonderful story; how far in literalness true is of no manner of moment to us; the myth, and power of it, *do* manifest the nature of the French kingdom, and prophesy its future destiny. Personal valour, personal beauty, loyalty to kings, love of women, disdain of unloving marriage, note all these things for true, and that in the corruption of these will be the last death of the Frank, as in their force was his first glory.

Personal valour, worth. *Utilitas*, the keystone of all. Birth nothing, except as gifting with valour ;—Law of primogeniture unknown ; —Propriety of conduct, it appears, for the present, also nowhere ! (but we are all pagans yet, remember).

12. Let us get our dates and our geography, at any rate, gathered out of the great 'nowhere' of confused memory, and set well together, thus far.

457. Merovée dies. The useful Childeric, counting his exile, and reign in Amiens, together, is King altogether twenty-four years, 457 to 481, and during his reign Odoacer ends the Roman empire in Italy, 476.

481. Clovis is only fifteen when he succeeds his father, as King of the Franks in Amiens. At this time a fragment of Roman power remains isolated in central France, while four strong and partly savage nations form a cross round this dying centre: the Frank on the north, the Breton on the west, the Burgundian on the east, the Visigoth, strongest of all and gentlest, in the south, from Loire to the sea.

Sketch for yourself, first, a map of France, as large as you like, as in Plate I.,* fig. 1,

* The first four figures in this illustration are explained in the text. The fifth represents the relations of Normandy, Maine, Anjou, and Aquitaine ; see Viollet Le Duc, 'Vict. Arch.,' vol. i., p. 136.

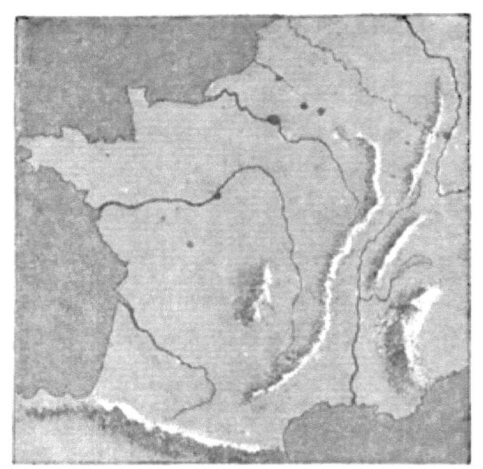

2

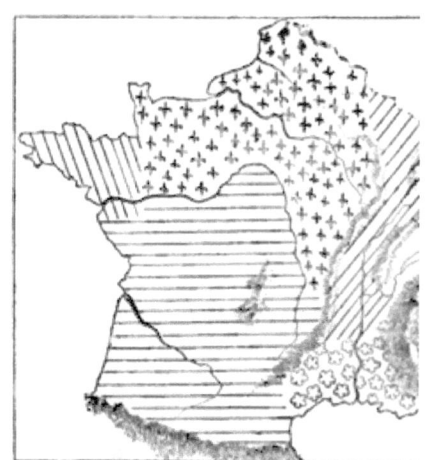

marking only the courses of the five rivers, Somme, Seine, Loire, Saone, Rhone; then, rudely, you find it was divided at the time thus, fig. 2 : Fleur - de - lysée part, Frank; \\\, Breton; ///, Burgundian; ≡, Visigoth. I am not sure how far these last reached across Rhone into Provence, but I think best to indicate Provence as semée with roses.

13. Now, under Clovis, the Franks fight three great battles. The first, with the Romans, near Soissons, which they win, and become masters of France as far as the Loire. Copy the rough map fig. 2, and put the fleur-de-lys all over the middle of it, extinguishing the Romans (fig. 3). This battle was won by Clovis, I believe, before he married Clotilde. He wins his princess by it: cannot get his pretty vase, however, to present to her. Keep that story well in your mind, and the battle of Soissons, as winning mid-France for the French, and ending the Romans there, for ever. Secondly, after he marries Clotilde, the wild Germans attack *him* from the north, and he has to fight for life and throne at Tolbiac. This is the battle in which he prays to the God of Clotilde, and quits himself of the

Germans by His help. Whereupon he is crowned in Rheims by St. Remy.

And now, in the new strength of his Christianity, and his twin victory over Rome and Germany, and his love for his queen, and his ambition for his people, he looks south on that vast Visigothic power, between Loire and the snowy mountains. Shall Christ, and the Franks, not be stronger than villainous Visigoths 'who are Arians also'? All his Franks are with him, in that opinion. So he marches against the Visigoths, meets them and their Alaric at Poitiers, ends their Alaric and their Arianism, and carries his faithful Franks to the Pic du Midi.

14. And so now you must draw the map of France once more, and put the fleur-de-lys all over its central mass from Calais to the Pyrenees: only Brittany still on the west, Burgundy in the east, and the white Provence rose beyond Rhone. And now poor little Amiens has become a mere border town like our Durham, and Somme a border streamlet like our Tyne. Loire and Seine have become the great French rivers, and men will be minded to build cities by these; where the

well-watered plains, not of peat, but richest pasture, may repose under the guard of saucy castles on the crags, and moated towers on the islands. But now let us think a little more closely what our changed symbols in the map may mean—five fleur-de-lys for level bar.

They don't mean, certainly, that all the Goths are gone, and nobody but Franks in France? The Franks have not massacred Visigothic man, woman, and child, from Loire to Garonne. Nay, where their own throne is still set by the Somme, the peat-bred people whom they found there, live there still, though subdued. Frank, or Goth, or Roman, may fluctuate hither and thither, in chasing or flying troops: but, unchanged through all the gusts of war, the rural people whose huts they pillage, whose farms they ravage, and over whose arts they reign, must still be diligently, silently, and with no time for lamentation, ploughing, sowing, cattle-breeding!

Else how could Frank or Hun, Visigoth or Roman, live for a month, or fight for a day?

15. Whatever the name, or the manners, of their masters, the ground delvers must be the same; and the goat-herd of the Pyrenees, and

the vine-dresser of Garonne, and the milkmaid of Picardy, give them what lords you may, abide in their land always, blossoming as the trees of the field, and enduring as the crags of the desert. And these, the warp and first substance of the nation, are divided, not by dynasties, but by climates; and are strong here, and helpless there, by privileges which no invading tyrants can abolish, and through faults which no preaching hermit can repress. Now, therefore, please let us leave our history a minute or two, and read the lessons of constant earth and sky.

16. In old times, when one posted from Calais to Paris, there was about half an hour's trot on the level, from the gate of Calais to the long chalk hill, which had to be climbed before arriving at the first post-house in the village of Marquise.

That chalk rise, virtually, is the front of France; that last bit of level north of it, virtually the last of Flanders; south of it, stretches now a district of chalk and fine building limestone,—(if you keep your eyes open, you may see a great quarry of it on the west of the railway, half-way between Calais and Boulogne, where once was a blessed little craggy dingle opening into velvet lawns ;)—this high, but never mountainous, calcareous tract, sweeping round the chalk basin of Paris away to Caen on one side, and Nancy on the other, and south as far as Bourges, and the Limousin. This limestone tract, with its keen fresh air, everywhere arable surface, and everywhere quarriable banks above well-watered meadow, is the real country of the French. Here only are their arts clearly developed. Farther south they are Gascons, or Limousins, or Auvergnats, or the like. Westward, grim-granitic Bretons; eastward, Alpine-bearish Burgundians: here only, on the chalk and finely-knit marble, between, say, Amiens and Chartres one way, and between Caen and Rheims on the other, have you real *France*.

17. Of which, before we carry on the farther vital history, I must ask the reader to consider with me a little, how history, so called, has been for the most part written, and of what particulars it usually consists.

Suppose that the tale of King Lear were a true one; and that a modern historian were giving the abstract of it in a school manual, purporting to contain all essential facts in British history valuable to British youth in competitive examination. The story would be related somewhat after this manner:—

"The reign of the last king of the seventy-ninth dynasty closed in a series of events with the record of which it is painful to pollute the pages of history. The weak old man wished to divide his kingdom into dowries for his three daughters; but on proposing this arrangement to them, finding it received by the youngest with coldness and reserve, he drove her from his court, and divided the kingdom between his two elder children.

"The youngest found refuge at the court of France, where ultimately the prince royal married her. But the two elder daughters, having obtained absolute power, treated their father at first with disrespect, and soon with contumely. Refused at last even the comforts necessary to his declining years, the old king, in a transport of rage, left the palace, with, it is said, only the court fool for an attendant, and wandered, frantic and half naked, during the storms of winter, in the woods of Britain.

18. "Hearing of these events, his youngest

daughter hastily collected an army, and invaded the territory of her ungrateful sisters, with the object of restoring her father to his throne: but, being met by a well-disciplined force, under the command of her eldest sister's paramour, Edmund, bastard son of the Earl of Gloucester, was herself defeated, thrown into prison, and soon afterwards strangled by the adulterer's order. The old king expired on receiving the news of her death; and the participators in these crimes soon after received their reward; for the two wicked queens being rivals for the affections of the bastard, the one of them who was regarded by him with less favour poisoned the other, and afterwards killed herself. Edmund afterwards met his death at the hand of his brother, the legitimate son of Gloucester, under whose rule, with that of the Earl of Kent, the kingdom remained for several succeeding years."

Imagine this succinctly graceful recital of what the historian conceived to be the facts, adorned with violently black and white woodcuts, representing the blinding of Gloucester, the phrenzy of Lear, the strangling of Cordelia, and the suicide of Goneril, and you have a type of popular history in the nineteenth century; which is, you may perceive after a little reflection, about as profitable reading for young persons (so far as regards the general colour and purity of their thoughts) as the Newgate Calendar would be; with this farther condition of incalculably greater evil, that, while the calendar of prison-crime would teach a thoughtful youth the dangers of low life and evil company, the calendar of kingly crime overthrows his respect for any manner of government, and his faith in the ordinances of Providence itself.

19. Books of loftier pretence, written by bankers, members of Parliament, or orthodox clergymen, are of course not wanting; and show that the progress of civilization consists in the victory of usury over ecclesiastical prejudice, or in the establishment of the Parliamentary privileges of the borough of Puddlecombe, or in the extinction of the benighted superstitions of the Papacy by the glorious light of Reformation. Finally, you have the broadly philosophical history, which proves to you that there is no evidence whatever of any overruling Providence in human

affairs; that all virtuous actions have selfish motives; and that a scientific selfishness, with proper telegraphic communications, and perfect knowledge of all the species of Bacteria, will entirely secure the future well-being of the upper classes of society, and the dutiful resignation of those beneath them.

Meantime, the two ignored powers—the Providence of Heaven, and the virtue of men —have ruled, and rule, the world, not invisibly; and they are the only powers of which history has ever to tell any profitable truth. Under all sorrow, there is the force of virtue; over all ruin, the restoring charity of God. To these alone we have to look; in these alone we may understand the past, and predict the future, destiny of the ages.

20. I return to the story of Clovis, king now of all central France. Fix the year 500 in your minds as the approximate date of his baptism at Rheims, and of St. Remy's sermon to him, telling him of the sufferings and passion of Christ, till Clovis sprang from his throne, grasping his spear, and crying, "Had I been there with my brave Franks, I would have avenged His wrongs."

"There is little doubt," proceeds the cockney historian, "that the conversion of Clovis was as much a matter of policy as of faith." But the cockney historian had better limit his remarks on the characters and faiths of men to those of the curates who have recently taken orders in his fashionable neighbourhood, or the bishops who have lately preached to the population of its manufacturing suburbs. Frankish kings were made of other clay.

21. The Christianity of Clovis does not indeed produce any fruits of the kind usually looked for in a modern convert. We do not hear of his repenting ever so little of any of his sins, nor resolving to lead a new life in any the smallest particular. He had not been impressed with convictions of sin at the battle of Tolbiac; nor, in asking for the help of the God of Clotilde, had he felt or professed the remotest intention of changing his character, or abandoning his projects. What he was, before he believed in his queen's God, he only more intensely afterwards became, in the confidence of that before unknown God's supernatural help. His natural gratitude to the

Delivering Power, and pride in its protection, added only fierceness to his soldiership, and deepened his political enmities with the rancour of religious indignation. No more dangerous snare is set by the fiends for human frailty than the belief that our own enemies are also the enemies of God; and it is perfectly conceivable to me that the conduct of Clovis might have been the more unscrupulous, precisely in the measure that his faith was more sincere.

Had either Clovis or Clotilde fully understood the precepts of their Master, the following history of France, and of Europe, would have been other than it is. What they could understand, or in any wise were taught, you will find that they obeyed, and were blessed in obeying. But their history is complicated with that of several other persons, respecting whom we must note now a few too much forgotten particulars.

22. If from beneath the apse of Amiens Cathedral we take the street leading due south, leaving the railroad-station on the left, it brings us to the foot of a gradually ascending hill, some half a mile long—a pleasant and quiet

walk enough, terminating on the level of the highest land near Amiens; whence, looking back, the Cathedral is seen beneath us, all but the flèche, our gained hill-top being on a level with its roof-ridge : and, to the south, the plain of France.

Somewhere about this spot, or in the line between it and St. Acheul, stood the ancient Roman gate of the Twins, whereon were Romulus and Remus being suckled by the wolf; and out of which, one bitter winter's day, a hundred and seventy years ago when Clovis was baptized—had ridden a Roman soldier, wrapped in his horseman's cloak,[5] on the causeway which was part of the great Roman road from Lyons to Boulogne.

23. And it is well worth your while also, some frosty autumn or winter day when the east wind is high, to feel the sweep of it at this spot, remembering what chanced here, memorable to all men, and serviceable, in that winter of the year 332, when men were dying for cold in Amiens streets :—namely, that the

---

[5] More properly, his knight's cloak ; in all likelihood the trabea, with purple and white stripes, dedicate to the kings of Rome, and chiefly to Romulus.

Roman horseman, scarce gone out of the city gate, was met by a naked beggar, shivering with cold; and that, seeing no other way of shelter for him, he drew his sword, divided his own cloak in two, and gave him half of it.

No ruinous gift, nor even enthusiastically generous: Sidney's cup of cold water needed more self-denial; and I am well assured that many a Christian child of our day, himself well warmed and clad, meeting one naked and cold, would be ready enough to give the *whole* cloak off his own shoulders to the necessitous one, if his better-advised nurse, or mamma, would let him. But this Roman soldier was no Christian, and did his serene charity in simplicity, yet with prudence.

Nevertheless, that same night, he beheld in a dream the Lord Jesus, who stood before him in the midst of angels, having on His shoulders the half of the cloak he had bestowed on the beggar.

And Jesus said to the angels that were around Him, "Know ye who hath thus arrayed me? My servant Martin, though yet unbaptized, has done this." And Martin after this vision hastened to receive baptism, being then in his twenty-third year.[6]

Whether these things ever were so, or how far so, credulous or incredulous reader, is no business whatever of yours or mine. What is, and shall be everlastingly, *so,*—namely, the infallible truth of the lesson herein taught, and the actual effect of the life of St. Martin on the mind of Christendom,—is, very absolutely, the business of every rational being in any Christian realm.

24. You are to understand, then, first of all, that the especial character of St. Martin is a serene and meek charity to all creatures. He is not a preaching saint—still less a persecuting one: not even an anxious one. Of his prayers we hear little—of his wishes, nothing. What he does always, is merely the right thing at the right moment;—rightness and kindness being in his mind one: an extremely exemplary saint, to my notion.

Converted and baptized—and conscious of having seen Christ—he nevertheless gives his officers no trouble whatever—does not try to make proselytes in his cohort. " It is Christ's

[6] Mrs. Jameson, Legendary Art, vol. ii., p. 721.

business, surely!—if He wants them, He may appear to them as He has to me," seems the feeling of his first baptized days. He remains seventeen years in the army, on those tranquil terms.

At the end of that time, thinking it might be well to take other service, he asks for his dismissal from the Emperor Julian,—on whose accusation of faint-heartedness, Martin offers, unarmed, to lead his cohort into battle, bearing only the sign of the cross. Julian takes him at his word,—keeps him in ward till time of battle comes; but, the day before he counts on putting him to that war ordeal, the barbarian enemy sends embassy with irrefusable offers of submission and peace.

25. The story is not often dwelt upon: how far literally true, again observe, does not in the least matter;—here *is* the lesson for ever given of the way in which a Christian soldier should meet his enemies. Which, had John Bunyan's Mr. Greatheart understood, the Celestial gates had opened by this time to many a pilgrim who has failed to hew his path up to them with the sword of sharpness.

But true in some practical and effectual way

the story *is;* for after a while, without any oratorizing, anathematizing, or any manner of disturbance, we find the Roman Knight made Bishop of Tours, and becoming an influence of unmixed good to all mankind, then, and afterwards. And virtually the same story is repeated of his bishop's robe as of his knight's cloak,—not to be rejected because so probable an invention; for it is just as probable an act.

26. Going, in his full robes, to say prayers in church, with one of his deacons, he came across some unhappily robeless person by the wayside; for whom he forthwith orders his deacon to provide some manner of coat, or gown.

The deacon objecting that no apparel of that profane nature is under his hand, St. Martin, with his customary serenity, takes off his own episcopal stole, or whatsoever flowing stateliness it might be, throws it on the destitute shoulders, and passes on to perform indecorous. public service in his waistcoat, or such mediæval nether attire as remained to him.

But, as he stood at the altar, a globe of light appeared above his head; and when he raised his bare arms with the Host—the angels were seen round him, hanging golden chains upon them, and jewels, not of the earth.

27. Incredible to you, in the nature of things, wise reader, and too palpably a gloss of monkish folly on the older story?

Be it so: yet in this fable of monkish folly, understood with the heart, would have been the chastisement and check of every form of the church's pride and sensuality, which in our day have literally sunk the service of God and His poor into the service of the clergyman and his rich; and changed what was once the garment of praise for the spirit of heaviness, into the spangling of Pantaloons in an ecclesiastical Masquerade.

28. But one more legend,—and we have enough to show us the roots of this saint's strange and universal power over Christendom.

"What peculiarly distinguished St. Martin was his sweet, serious, unfailing serenity; no one had ever seen him angry, or sad, or gay; there was nothing in his heart but piety to God and pity for men. The Devil, who was particularly envious of his virtues, detested above all his exceeding charity, because it was the most inimical to his own power, and one

C

day reproached him mockingly that he so soon received into favour the fallen and the repentant. But St. Martin answered him sorrowfully, saying, 'Oh most miserable that thou art! if *thou* also couldst cease to persecute and seduce wretched men, if thou also couldst repent, thou also shouldst find mercy and forgiveness through Jesus Christ.' "[7]

29. In this gentleness was his strength; and the issue of it is best to be estimated by comparing its scope with that of the work of St. Firmin. The impatient missionary riots and rants about Amiens' streets—insults, exhorts, persuades, baptizes,—turns everything, as aforesaid, upside down for forty days: then gets his head cut off, and is never more named, *out* of Amiens. St. Martin teazes nobody, spends not a breath in unpleasant exhortation, understands, by Christ's first lesson to himself, that undipped people may be as good as dipped if their hearts are clean ; helps, forgives, and cheers, (companionable even to the loving-cup,) as readily the clown as the king; he is the patron of honest drinking ; the stuffing of your Martinmas goose is fragrant in his nostrils, and

[7] Mrs. Jameson, vol. ii., p. 722.

sacred to him the last kindly rays of departing summer. And somehow — the idols totter before him far and near—the Pagan gods fade, *his* Christ becomes all men's Christ—his name is named over new shrines innumerable in all lands; high on the Roman hills, lowly in English fields;—St. Augustine, baptized his first English converts in St. Martin's church at Canterbury; and the Charing Cross station itself has not yet effaced wholly from London minds his memory or his name.

30. That story of the Episcopal Robe is the last of St. Martin respecting which I venture to tell you that it is wiser to suppose it literally true than a *mere* myth ; myth, however, of the deepest value and beauty it remains assuredly : and this really last story I have to tell, which I admit you will be wiser in thinking a fable than exactly true, nevertheless had assuredly at its root some grain of fact (sprouting a hundred-fold) cast on good ground by a visible and unforgetable piece of St. Martin's actual behaviour in high company ; while, as a myth, it is every whit and for ever valuable and comprehensive.

St. Martin, then, as the tale will have it, was

dining one day at the highest of tables in the terrestrial globe—namely, with the Emperor and Empress of Germany! You need not inquire what Emperor, or which of the Emperor's wives! The Emperor of Germany is, in all early myths, the expression for the highest sacred power of the State, as the Pope is the highest sacred power of the Church. St. Martin was dining then, as aforesaid, with the Emperor, of course sitting next him on his left—Empress opposite on his right: everything orthodox. St. Martin much enjoying his dinner, and making himself generally agreeable to the company: not in the least a John Baptist sort of a saint. You are aware also that in Royal feasts in those days persons of much inferior rank in society were allowed in the hall: got behind people's chairs, and saw and heard what was going on, while they unobtrusively picked up crumbs, and licked trenchers.

When the dinner was a little forward, and time for wine came, the Emperor fills his own cup—fills the Empress's—fills St. Martin's,—affectionately hobnobs with St. Martin. The equally loving, and yet more truly believing,

Empress, looks across the table, humbly, but also royally, expecting St. Martin, of course, next to hobnob with *her*. St. Martin looks round, first, deliberately ;—becomes aware of a tatterdemalion and thirsty-looking soul of a beggar at his chair side, who has managed to get *his* cup filled somehow, also—by a charitable lacquey.

St. Martin turns his back on the Empress, and hobnobs with *him!*

31. For which charity—mythic if you like, but evermore exemplary—he remains, as aforesaid, the patron of good-Christian topers to this hour.

As gathering years told upon him, he seems to have felt that he had carried weight of crozier long enough—that busy Tours must now find a busier Bishop—that, for himself, he might innocently henceforward take his pleasure and his rest where the vine grew and the lark sang. For his episcopal palace, he takes a little cave in the chalk cliffs of the up-country river: arranges all matters therein, for bed and board, at small cost. Night by night the stream murmurs to him, day by day the vine-leaves give their shade; and, daily by the horizon's breadth so much nearer Heaven, the fore-running sun goes down for him beyond the glowing water;—there, where now the peasant woman trots homewards between her panniers, and the saw rests in the half-cleft wood, and the village spire rises grey against the farthest light, in Turner's 'Loireside.'[8]

32. All which things, though not themselves without profit, my special reason for telling you now, has been that you might understand the significance of what chanced first on Clovis' march south against the Visigoths.

Having passed the Loire at Tours, he traversed the lands of the abbey of St. Martin, which he declared inviolate, and refused permission to his soldiers to touch anything, save water and grass for their horses. So rigid were his orders, and the obedience he exacted in this respect, that a Frankish soldier having taken, without the consent of the owner, some hay which belonged to a poor man, saying in raillery "that it was but grass," he caused the aggressor to be put to death, exclaiming that "Victory could not be expected, if St. Martin should be offended."

[8] Modern Painters, Plate 73.

33. Now, mark you well, this passage of the Loire at Tours is virtually the fulfilment of the proper bounds of the French kingdom, and the sign of its approved and securely set power is " Honour to the poor!" Even a little grass is not to be stolen from a poor man, on pain of Death. So wills the Christian knight of Roman armies; throned now high with God. So wills the first Christian king of far victorious Franks;—here baptized to God in Jordan of his goodly land, as he goes over to possess it.

How long?

Until that same Sign should be read backwards from a degenerate throne;—until, message being brought that the poor of the French people had no bread to eat, answer should be returned to them " They may eat grass." Whereupon—by St. Martin's faubourg, and St. Martin's gate—there go forth commands from the Poor Man's Knight against the King—which end *his* feasting.

And be this much remembered by you, of the power over French souls, past and to come, of St. Martin of Tours.

NOTES TO CHAPTER I.

34. THE reader will please observe that notes immediately necessary to the understanding of the text will be given, with *numbered* references, under the text itself; while questions of disputing authorities, or quotations of supporting documents, will have *lettered* references, and be thrown together at the end of each chapter. One good of this method * will be that, after the numbered notes are all right, if I see need of farther explanation, as I revise the press, I can insert a letter referring to a *final* note without confusion of the standing types. There will be some use also in the final notes, in summing the chapters, or saying what is to be more carefully remembered of them. Thus just now it is of no consequence to remember that the first taking of Amiens was in 445, because that is not the founding of the Merovingian dynasty; neither that Merovæus seized the throne in 447 and died ten years later. The real date to be remembered is 481, when Clovis himself comes to the throne, a boy of fifteen; and the three battles of Clovis' reign to be remembered are Soissons,

* This method is not, however, followed in the succeeding chapters.—ED. (1897).

Tolbiac, and Poitiers—remembering also that this was the first of the three great battles of Poitiers;—how the Poitiers district came to have such importance as a battle-position, we must afterwards discover if we can. Of Queen Clotilde and her flight from Burgundy to her Frank lover we must hear more in next chapter,—the story of the vase at Soissons is given in "The Pictorial History of France," but must be deferred also, with such comment as it needs, to next chapter; for I wish the reader's mind, in the close of this first number, to be left fixed on two descriptions of the modern 'Frank' (taking that word in its Saracen sense), as distinguished from the modern Saracen. The first description is by Colonel Butler, entirely true and admirable, except in the implied extension of the contrast to olden time: for the Saxon soul under Alfred, the Teutonic under Charlemagne, and the Frank under St. Louis, were quite as religious as any Asiatic's, though more practical; it is only the modern mob of kingless miscreants in the West, who have sunk themselves by gambling, swindling, machine-making, and gluttony, into the scurviest louts that have ever fouled the Earth with the carcases she lent them.

35. "Of the features of English character brought to light by the spread of British dominion in Asia, there is nothing more observable than the contrast between the religious bias of Eastern thought and the innate absence of religion in

the Anglo-Saxon mind. Turk and Greek, Buddhist and Armenian, Copt and Parsee, all manifest in a hundred ways of daily life the great fact of their belief in a God. In their vices as well as in their virtues the recognition of Deity is dominant.

"With the Western, on the contrary, the outward form of practising belief in a God is a thing to be half-ashamed of—something to hide. A procession of priests in the Strada Reale would probably cause an average Briton to regard it with less tolerant eye than he would cast upon a Juggernaut festival in Orissa : but to each alike would he display the same iconoclasm of creed, the same idea, not the less fixed because it is seldom expressed in words : 'You pray ; therefore I do not think much of you.' But there is a deeper difference between East and West lying beneath this incompatibility of temper on the part of modern Englishmen to accept the religious habit of thought in the East. All Eastern peoples possess this habit of thought. It is the one tie which links together their widely differing races. Let us give an illustration of our meaning. On an Austrian Lloyd's steamboat in the Levant a traveller from Beyrout will frequently see strange groups of men crowded together on the quarterdeck. In the morning the missal books of the Greek Church will be laid along the bulwarks of the ship, and a couple of Russian priests, coming from Jerusalem, will be busy muttering mass. A yard to right or left a Turkish pilgrim, returning from Mecca, sits a respectful observer of the scene. It is prayer, and therefore it is holy in his sight. So, too, when the evening hour has come, and the Turk spreads out his bit of carpet for the sunset prayers and obeisance towards Mecca, the Greek looks on in silence, without trace of scorn in his face, for it is again the worship of the Creator by the created. They are both fulfilling the *first* law of the East—prayer to God; and whether the shrine be Jerusalem, Mecca, or Lhassa, the sanctity of worship surrounds the votary, and protects the pilgrim.

"Into this life comes the Englishman, frequently destitute of one touch of sympathy with the prayers of any people, or the faith of any creed; hence our rule in the East has ever rested, and will ever rest, upon the bayonet. We have never yet got beyond the stage of conquest; never assimilated a people to our ways, never even civilised a single tribe around the wide dominion of our empire. It is curious how frequently a well-meaning Briton will speak of a foreign church or temple as though it had presented itself to his mind in the same light in which the City of London appeared to Blucher —as something to loot. The other idea, that a priest was a person to hang, is one which is also often observable in the British brain. On one occasion, when we were endeavouring to enlighten our minds on the Greek question, as it had presented itself to a naval officer whose vessel had been stationed in Greek and Adriatic waters during our occupation of Corfu and the other Ionian Isles, we could only elicit from our informant the fact that one morning before breakfast he had hanged seventeen priests."

36. The second passage which I store in these notes for future use, is the supremely magnificent one, out of a book full of magnificence,—if truth be counted as having in it the strength of deed: Alphonse Karr's "Grains de Bon Sens." I cannot praise either this or his more recent "Bourdonnements" to my own heart's content, simply because they are by a man utterly after my own heart, who has been saying in France, this many a year, what I also, this many a year, have been saying in England, neither of us knowing of the other, and both of us vainly. (See pages 11 and 12 of "Bourdonnements.") The passage here given is the sixty-third clause in "Grains de Bon Sens."

"Et tout cela, monsieur, vient de ce qu'il n'y a plus de croyances—de ce qu'on ne croit plus à rien.

"Ah! saperlipopette, monsieur, vous me la baillez belle! Vous dites qu'on ne croit plus à rien! Mais jamais, à aucune époque, on n'a cru à tant de billevesées, de bourdes, de mensonges, de sottises, d'absurdités qu'aujourd'hui.

"D'abord, on *croit* à l'incrédulité—l'incrédulité est une croyance, une religion trés exigeante, qui a ses dogmes, sa liturge, ses pratiques, ses rites! . . . son intolérance, ses superstitions. Nous avons des incrédules et des impies Jésuites, et des incrédules et des impies jansénistes ; des impies molinistes, et des impies quiétistes ; des impies pratiquants, et non pratiquants ; des impies indifférents et des impies fanatiques ; des incrédules cagots et des impies hypocrites et tartuffes.—La religion de l'incrédulité ne se refuse même pas le luxe des hérésies.

"On ne croit plus à la bible, je le veux bien, mais on *croit* aux 'écritures' des journaux, on croit au 'sacerdoce' des gazettes et carrés de papier, et à leurs 'oracles' quotidiens.

"On *croit* au 'baptême' de la police correctionnelle et de la Cour d'assises — on appelle 'martyrs' et 'confesseurs' les 'absents' à Nouméa et les 'frères' de Suisse, d'Angleterre et de Belgique—et, quand on parle des 'martyrs de la Commune,' ça ne s'entend pas des assassinés, mais des assassins.

"On se fait enterrer 'civilement,' on ne veut plus sur son cercueil des prières de l'Eglise, on ne veut ni cierges, ni chants religieux,—mais on veut un cortège portant derrière la bière des immortelles rouges ;—on veut une 'oraison,' une 'prédication' de Victor Hugo qui a ajouté cette spécialité à ses autres spécialités, si bien qu'un de ces jours derniers, comme il suivait un convoi en amateur, un croque-mort s'approcha de lui, le poussa du coude, et lui dit en souriant : 'Est-ce que nous n'aurons pas quelque chose de vous, aujourd'hui ?'—Et cette prédication il la lit ou la récite— ou, s'il ne juge pas à propos 'd'officier' lui-même, s'il s'agit d'un mort de plus, il envoie pour la psalmodier M. Meurice ou tout autre 'prêtre' ou 'enfant de cœur' du 'Dieu.'—A défaut de M. Hugo, s'il s'agit d'un citoyen obscur, on se contente d'une homélie improvisée pour la dixième fois par n'importe quel député intransigeant—et le *Miserere* est remplacé par les cris de 'Vive la République!' poussés dans le cimetière.

"On n'entre plus dans les églises, mais on fréquente les brasseries et les cabarets; on y officie, on y célèbre les mystères, on y chante les louanges d'une prétendue république *sacro-sainte*, une, indivisible, démocratique, sociale, athénienne, intransigeante, despotique, invisible quoique étant partout. On y communie sous différentes espèces; le matin (*matines*) on 'tue le ver' avec le vin blanc,—il y a plus tard les vêpres de l'absinthe, auxquelles on se ferait un crime de manquer d'assiduité.

"On ne croit plus en Dieu, mais on *croit* pieusement en M. Gambetta, en MM. Marcou, Naquet, Barodet, Tartempion, etc., et en toute une longue litanie de saints et de *dii minores* tels que Goutte-Noire, Polosse, Boriasse et Silibat, le héros lyonnais.

"On *croit* à 'l'immuabilité' de M. Thiers, qui a dit avec aplomb 'Je ne change jamais,' et qui aujourd'hui est à la fois le protecteur et le protégé de ceux qu'il a passé une partie de sa vie à fusiller, et qu'il fusillait encore hier.

"On *croit* au républicanisme 'immaculé' de l'avocat de Cahors qui a jeté par-dessus bord tous les principes républicains,—qui est à la fois de son côté le protecteur et le protégé de M. Thiers, qui hier l'appelait 'fou furieux,' déportait et fusillait ses amis.

"Tous deux, il est vrai, en même temps protecteurs hypocrites, et protégés dupés.

"On ne croit plus aux miracles anciens, mais on *croit* à des miracles nouveaux.

"On *croit* à une république sans le respect religieux et presque fanatique des lois.

"On *croit* qu'on peut s'enrichir en restant imprévoyants, insouciants et paresseux, et autrement que par le travail et l'économie.

"On se *croit* libre en obéissant aveuglément et bêtement à deux ou trois coteries.

"On se *croit* indépendant parce qu'on a tué ou chassé un lion, et qu'on l'a remplacé par deux douzaines de caniches teints en jaune.

"On *croit* avoir conquis le 'suffrage universel' en votant par des mots d'ordre qui en font le contraire du suffrage universel,—mené au vote comme on mène un troupeau au pâturage, avec cette différence que ça ne nourrit pas.—D'ailleurs, par ce suffrage universel qu'on croit avoir et qu'on n'a pas,—il faudrait *croire* que les soldats doivent commander au général, les chevaux mener le cocher;—*croire* que deux radis valent mieux qu'une truffe, deux cailloux mieux qu'un diamant, deux crottins mieux qu'une rose.

"On se *croit* en République, parce que quelques demi-quarterons de farceurs occupent les mêmes places, émargent les mêmes appointements, pratiquent les mêmes abus, que ceux qu'on a renversés à leur bénéfice.

"On se *croit* un peuple opprimé, héroïque, que brise ses fers, et n'est qu'un domestique capricieux qui aime à changer de maîtres.

"On *croit* au génie d'avocats de sixième ordre, qui ne se sont jetés dans la politique et n'aspirent au gouvernement despotique de la France que faute d'avoir pu gagner honnêtement, sans grand travail, dans l'exercice d'une profession correcte, une vie obscure humectée de chopes.

"On *croit* que des hommes dévoyés, déclassés, décavés, fruits secs, etc., qui n'ont étudié que le 'domino à quatre' et le 'bezigue en quinze cents' se réveillent un matin,—après un sommeil alourdi par le tabac et la bière—possédant la science de la politique, et l'art de la guerre ; et aptes à être dictateurs, généraux, ministres, préfets, sous-préfets, etc.

"Et les soi-distant conservateurs eux-mêmes *croient* que la France peut se relever et vivre tant qu'on n'aura pas fait justice de ce prétendu suffrage universel qui est le contraire du suffrage universel.

"Les croyances ont subi le sort de ce serpent de la fable—coupé, haché par morceaux, dont chaque tronçon devenait un serpent.

"Les croyances se sont changées en monnaie— en billon de crédulités.

"Et pour finir la liste bien incomplète des croyances et des crédulités—vous *croyez*, vous, qu'on ne croit à rien !"

II. AMIENS.
Northern Porch before Restoration.

CHAPTER II.

UNDER THE DRACHENFELS.

1. WITHOUT ignobly trusting the devices of artificial memory—far less slighting the pleasure and power of resolute and thoughtful memory — my younger readers will find it extremely useful to note any coincidences or links of number which may serve to secure in their minds what may be called Dates of Anchorage, round which others, less important, may swing at various cables' lengths.

Thus, it will be found primarily a most simple and convenient arrangement of the years since the birth of Christ, to divide them by fives of centuries,—that is to say, by the marked periods of the fifth, tenth, fifteenth, and, now fast nearing us, twentieth centuries.

And this — at first seemingly formal and arithmetical—division, will be found, as we use it, very singularly emphasized by signs of most notable change in the knowledge, disciplines, and morals of the human race.

2. All dates, it must farther be remembered, falling within the fifth century, begin with the number 4 (401, 402, etc.); and all dates in the tenth century with the number 9 (901, 902, etc.); and all dates in the fifteenth century with the number 14 (1401, 1402, etc.).

In our immediate subject of study, we are concerned with the first of these marked centuries—the fifth—of which I will therefore ask you to observe two very interesting divisions.

All dates of years in that century, we said, must begin with the number 4.

If you halve it for the second figure, you get 42.

And if you double it for the second figure, you get 48.

Add 1, for the third figure, to each of these numbers, and you get 421 and 481, which two dates you will please fasten well down, and let there be no drifting about of them in your heads.

For the first is the date of the birth of Venice herself, and her dukedom, (see 'St.

Mark's Rest,' Part I., p. 30); and the second is the date of birth of the French Venice, and her kingdom; Clovis being in that year crowned in Amiens.

3. These are the great Birthdays—Birthdates—in the fifth century, of Nations. Its Deathdays we will count, at another time.

Since, not for dark Rialto's dukedom, nor for fair France's kingdom, only, are these two years to be remembered above all others in the wild fifth century; but because they are also the birth-years of a great Lady, and greater Lord, of all future Christendom—St. Genevieve, and St. Benedict.

Genevieve, the 'white wave' (Laughing water)—the purest of all the maids that have been named from the sea-foam or the rivulet's ripple, unsullied,—not the troubled and troubling Aphrodite, but the Leucothea of Ulysses, the guiding wave of deliverance.

White wave on the blue—whether of pure lake or sunny sea—(thenceforth the colours of France, blue field with white lilies), she is always the type of purity, in active brightness of the entire soul and life—(so distinguished from the quieter and restricted innocence of

St. Agnes),—and all the traditions of sorrow in the trial or failure of noble womanhood are connected with her name; Ginevra, in Italian, passing into Shakespeare's Imogen; and Guinevere, the torrent wave of the British mountain streams, of whose pollution your modern sentimental minstrels chant and moan to you, lugubriously useless;—but none tell you, that I hear, of the victory and might of this white wave of France.

4. A shepherd maid she was—a tiny thing, barefooted, bareheaded—such as you may see running wild and innocent, less cared for now than their sheep, over many a hillside of France and Italy. Tiny enough;—seven years old, all told, when first one hears of her: "Seven times one are seven, (I am old, you may trust me, linnet, linnet*)," and all around her—fierce as the Furies, and wild as the winds of heaven—the thunder of the Gothic armies reverberate over the ruins of the world.

5. Two leagues from Paris, (*Roman* Paris, soon to pass away with Rome herself,) the little thing keeps her flock, not even her own, nor her father's flock, like David; she is the

---

* Miss Ingelow.

hired servant of a richer farmer of Nanterre. Who can tell me anything about Nanterre?— which of our pilgrims of this omni-speculant, omni-nescient age has thought of visiting what shrine may be there? I don't know even on what side of Paris it lies,* nor under which heap of railway cinders and iron one is to conceive the sheep-walks and blossomed fields of fairy Saint Phyllis. There were such left, even in my time, between Paris and St. Denis, (see the prettiest chapter in all the "Mysteries of Paris" where Fleur de Marie runs wild in them for the first time), but now, I suppose, Saint Phyllis's native earth is all thrown up into bastion and glacis, (profitable and blessed of all saints, and her, as *these* have since proved themselves!), or else are covered with manufactories and cabarets. Seven years old she was, then, when on his way to *England* from Auxerre, St. Germain passed a night in her village, and among the children who brought him on his way in the morning in more kindly manner than Elisha's convoy, noticed this one—wider-eyed in reverence than the rest; drew her to him, questioned her, and was

* On inquiry, I find in the flat between Paris and Sèvres.

sweetly answered That she would fain be Christ's handmaid. And he hung round her neck a small copper coin, marked with the cross. Thenceforward Genevieve held herself as "separated from the world."

6. It did not turn out so, however. Far the contrary. You must think of her, instead, as the first of Parisiennes. Queen of Vanity Fair, that was to be, sedately poor St. Phyllis, with her copper-crossed farthing about her neck! More than Nitocris was to Egypt, more than Semiramis to Nineveh, more than Zenobia to the city of palm trees—this seven-years-old shepherd maiden became to Paris and her France. You have not heard of her in that kind?—No: how should you?—for she did not lead armies, but stayed them, and all her power was in peace.

7. There are, however, some seven or eight and twenty lives of her, I believe; into the literature of which I cannot enter, nor need, all having been ineffective in producing any clear picture of her to the modern French or English mind; and leaving one's own poor sagacities and fancy to gather and shape the sanctity of her into an intelligible, I do not say

a *credible*, form; for there is no question here about belief,—the creature is as real as Joan of Arc, and far more powerful;—she is separated, just as St. Martin is, by his patience, from too provocative prelates—by her quietness of force, from the pitiable crowd of feminine martyr saints.

There are thousands of religious girls who have never got themselves into any calendars, but have wasted and wearied away their lives —heaven knows why, for *we* cannot; but here is one, at any rate, who neither scolds herself to martyrdom, nor frets herself into consumption, but becomes a tower of the Flock, and builder of folds for them all her days.

8. The first thing, then, you have to note of her, is that she is a pure native *Gaul*. She does not come as a missionary out of Hungary, or Illyria, or Egypt, or ineffable space; but grows at Nanterre, like a marguerite in the dew, the first " Reine Blanche " of Gaul.

I have not used this ugly word 'Gaul' before, and we must be quite sure what it means, at once, though it will cost us a long parenthesis.

9. During all the years of the rising power

of Rome, her people called everybody a Gaul who lived north of the sources of Tiber. If you are not content with that general statement, you may read the article "Gallia" in Smith's dictionary, which consists of seventy-one columns of close print, containing each as much as three of my pages; and tells you at the end of it, that "though long, it is not complete." You may, however, gather from it, after an attentive perusal, as much as I have above told you.

But, as early as the second century after Christ, and much more distinctly in the time with which we are ourselves concerned—the fifth—the wild nations opposed to Rome, and partially subdued, or held at bay by her, had resolved themselves into two distinct masses, belonging to two distinct *latitudes*. One, *fixed* in habitation of the pleasant temperate zone of Europe—England with her western mountains, the healthy limestone plateaux and granite mounts of France, the German labyrinths of woody hill and winding thal, from the Tyrol to the Hartz, and all the vast enclosed basin and branching valleys of the Carpathians. Think of these four districts, briefly and clearly, as 'Britain,' 'Gaul,' 'Germany,' and 'Dacia.'

10. North of these rudely but patiently *resident* races, possessing fields and orchards, quiet herds, homes of a sort, moralities and memories not ignoble, dwelt, or rather drifted, and shook, a shattered chain of gloomier tribes, piratical mainly, and predatory, nomad essentially; homeless, of necessity, finding no stay nor comfort in earth, or bitter sky: desperately wandering along the waste sands and drenched morasses of the flat country stretching from the mouths of the Rhine to those of the Vistula, and beyond Vistula nobody knows where, nor needs to know. Waste sands and rootless bogs their portion, ice-fastened and cloud-shadowed, for many a day of the rigorous year: shallow pools and oozings and windings of retarded streams, black decay of neglected woods, scarcely habitable, never loveable; to this day the inner mainlands little changed for good *—and their inhabitants now fallen even on sadder times.

* See generally any description that Carlyle has had occasion to give of Prussian or Polish ground, or edge of Baltic shore.

11. For in the fifth century they had herds of cattle* to drive and kill, unpreserved hunting-grounds full of game and wild deer, tameable reindeer also then, even so far in the south; spirited hogs, good for practice of fight as in Meleager's time, and afterwards for bacon; furry creatures innumerable, all good for meat or skin. Fish of the infinite sea breaking their back-fibre nets; fowl innumerable, migrant in the skies, for their flint-headed arrows; bred horses for their own riding; ships of no mean size, and of all sorts, flat-bottomed for the oozy puddles, keeled and decked for strong Elbe stream and furious Baltic on the one side,—for mountain-cleaving Danube and the black lake of Colchos on the south.

12. And they were, to all outward aspect, and in all *felt* force, the living powers of the world, in that long hour of its transfiguration. All else known once for awful, had become formalism, folly, or shame:—the Roman armies,

---

* Gigantic—and not yet fossilized! See Gibbon's note on the death of Theodebert: "The King pointed his spear —the Bull *overturned a tree on his head*,—he died the same day."—vii. 255. The Horn of Uri and her shield, with the chiefly towering crests of the German helm, attest the terror of these Aurochs herds.

a mere sworded mechanism, fast falling confused, every sword against its fellow;—the Roman civil multitude, mixed of slaves, slave-masters, and harlots; the East, cut off from Europe by the intervening weakness of the Greek. These starving troops of the Black forests and White seas, themselves half wolf, half drift-wood, (as *we* once called ourselves Lion-hearts, and Oak-hearts, so they), merciless as the herded hound, enduring as the wild birch-tree and pine. You will hear of few beside them for five centuries yet to come: Visigoths, west of Vistula;—Ostrogoths, east of Vistula; radiant round little Holy Island (Heligoland), our own Saxons, and Hamlet the Dane, and his foe the sledded Polack on the ice,—all these south of Baltic; and, pouring *across* Baltic, constantly, her mountain-ministered strength, Scandinavia, until at last *she* for a time rules all, and the Norman name is of disputeless dominion, from the North Cape to Jerusalem.

13. *This* is the apparent, this the only recognised world history, as I have said, for five centuries to come. And yet the real history is underneath all this. The wandering

armies are, in the heart of them, only living hail, and thunder, and fire along the ground. But the Suffering Life, the rooted heart of native humanity, growing up in eternal gentleness, howsoever wasted, forgotten, or spoiled, —itself neither wasting, nor wandering, nor slaying, but unconquerable by grief or death, became the seed ground of all love, that was to be born in due time ; giving, then, to mortality, what hope, joy, or genius it could receive; and—if there be immortality—rendering out of the grave to the Church her fostering Saints, and to Heaven her helpful Angels.

14. Of this low-nestling, speechless, harmless, infinitely submissive, infinitely serviceable order of being, no Historian ever takes the smallest notice, except when it is robbed, or slain. I can give you no picture of it, bring to your ears no murmur of it, nor cry. I can only show you the absolute 'must have been' of its unrewarded past, and the way in which all we have thought of, or been told, is founded on the deeper facts in its history, unthought of, and untold.

15. The main mass of this innocent and invincible peasant life is, as I have above told

you, grouped in the fruitful and temperate districts of (relatively) mountainous Europe,—reaching, west to east, from the Cornish Land's End to the mouth of the Danube. Already, in the times we are now dealing with, it was full of native passion—generosity—and intelligence capable of all things. Dacia gave to Rome the four last of her great Emperors,*—Britain to Christianity the first deeds, and the final legends, of her chivalry,—Germany, to all manhood, the truth and the fire of the Frank,—Gaul, to all womanhood, the patience and strength of St. Genevieve.

16. The *truth*, and the fire, of the Frank,—I must repeat with insistance,—for my younger readers have probably been in the habit of thinking that the French were more polite than true. They will find, if they examine

---

* Claudius, Aurelian, Probus, Constantius; and after the division of the empire, to the East, Justinian. "The emperor Justinian was born of an obscure race of Barbarians, the inhabitants of a wild and desolate country, to which the names of Dardania, of Dacia, and of Bulgaria have been successively applied. The names of these Dardanian peasants are Gothic, and almost English. Justinian is a translation of Uprauder (upright); his father, Sabatius,—in Græco-barbarous language, Stipes—was styled in his village 'Istock' (Stock)."—Gibbon, beginning of chap. xl. and note.

into the matter, that only Truth *can* be polished: and that all we recognize of beautiful, subtle, or constructive, in the manners, the language, or the architecture of the French, comes of a pure veracity in their nature, which you will soon feel in the living creatures themselves if you love them : if you understand even their worst rightly, their very Revolution was a revolt against lies ; and against the betrayal of Love. No people had ever been so loyal in vain.

17. That they were originally Germans, they themselves I suppose would now gladly forget; but how they shook the dust of Germany off their feet—and gave themselves a new name—is the first of the phenomena which we have now attentively to observe respecting them.

"The most rational critics," says Mr. Gibbon in his tenth chapter, "*suppose* that *about* the year 240" (*suppose* then, we, for our greater comfort, say *about* the year 250, half-way to end of fifth century, where we are,—ten years less or more, in cases of 'supposing about,' do not much matter, but some floating buoy of a date will be handy here.)

'About' A.D. 250, then, " a new confederacy was formed under the name of Franks, by the old inhabitants of the lower Rhine and the Weser."

18. My own impression, concerning the old inhabitants of the lower Rhine and the Weser, would have been that they consisted mostly of fish, with superficial frogs and ducks; but Mr. Gibbon's note on the passage informs us that the new confederation composed itself of human creatures, in these items following—

1. The Chauci, who lived we are not told where.
2. The Sicambri ,, in the Principality of Waldeck.
3. The Attuarii ,, in the Duchy of Berg.
4. The Bructeri ,, on the banks of the Lippe.
5. The Chamavii ,, in the country of the Bructeri.
6. The Catti ,, in Hessia.

All this I believe you will be rather easier in your minds if you forget than if you remember; but if it please you to read, or re-read, (or best of all, get read to you by some real Miss Isabella Wardour,) the story of Martin Waldeck in the 'Antiquary,' you will gain from it a sufficient notion of the central character of "the Principality of *Waldeck*" connected securely with that important German word; 'woody'—or 'wood*ish*,' I suppose?—descriptive of rock and half-grown forest; together with some wholesome reverence for Scott's instinctively deep foundations of nomenclature.

19. But for our present purpose we must also take seriously to our maps again, and get things within linear limits of space.

All the maps of Germany which I have myself the privilege of possessing, diffuse themselves, just north of Frankfort, into the likeness of a painted window broken small by Puritan malice, and put together again by ingenious churchwardens with every bit of it wrong side upwards;—this curious vitreric purporting to represent the sixty, seventy, eighty, or ninety dukedoms, marquisates, counties, baronies, electorates, and the like, into which hereditary Alemannia cracked itself in that latitude. But under the mottling colours, and through the jotted and jumbled alphabets of distracted dignities—besides a chain-mail of black railroads over all, the chains of it not in links, but bristling with legs, like centipedes,—a hard forenoon's work with good magnifying-glass enables one approximately to make out the course of the Weser, and the names of certain towns near its sources, deservedly memorable.

20. In case you have not a forenoon to spare, nor eyesight to waste, this much of merely necessary abstract must serve you,—that from the Drachenfels and its six brother felsen, eastward, trending to the north, there runs and spreads a straggling company of gnarled and mysterious craglets, jutting and scowling above glens fringed by coppice, and fretful or musical with stream: the crags, in pious ages, mostly castled, for distantly or fancifully Christian purposes;—the glens, resonant of woodmen, or burrowed at the sides by miners, and invisibly tenanted farther, underground, by gnomes, and above by forest and other demons. The entire district, clasping crag to crag, and guiding dell to dell, some hundred and fifty miles (with intervals) between the Dragon mountain above Rhine, and the Rosin mountain, 'Hartz' shadowy still to the south of the riding grounds of Black Brunswickers of indisputable bodily presence;—shadowy anciently with 'Hercynian' (hedge, or fence) forest, corrupted or coinciding into Hartz, or

Rosin forest, haunted by obscurely apparent foresters of at least resinous, not to say sulphurous, extraction.

21. A hundred and fifty miles east to west, say half as much north to south—about a thousand square miles in whole—of metalliferous, coniferous, and Ghostiferous mountain, fluent, and diffluent for us, both in mediæval and recent times, with the most Essential oil of Turpentine, and Myrrh or Frankincense of temper and imagination, which may be typified by it, producible in Germany;—especially if we think how the more delicate uses of Rosin, as indispensable to the Fiddle-bow, have developed themselves, from the days of St. Elizabeth of Marburg to those of St. Mephistopheles of Weimar.

22. As far as I know, this cluster of wayward cliff and dingle has no common name as a group of hills; and it is quite impossible to make out the diverse branching of it in any maps I can lay hand on: but we may remember easily, and usefully, that it is *all* north of the Maine,—that it rests on the Drachenfels at one end, and tosses itself away to the morning light with a concave

swoop, up to the Hartz, (Brocken summit, 3,700 feet above sea, nothing higher): with one notable interval for Weser stream, of which presently.

23. We will call this, in future, the chain, or company, of the Enchanted Mountains; and then we shall all the more easily join on the Giant mountains, Riesen-Gebirge, when we want them: but these are altogether higher, sterner, and not yet to be invaded; the nearer ones, through which our road lies, we might perhaps more patly call the Goblin mountains; but that would be scarcely reverent to St. Elizabeth, nor to the numberless pretty chatelaines of towers, and princesses of park and glen, who have made German domestic manners sweet and exemplary, and have led their lightly rippling and translucent lives down the glens of ages, until enchantment becomes, perhaps, too canonical, in the Almanach de Gotha.

We will call them therefore the Enchanted Mountains, not the Goblin; perceiving gratefully also that the Rock spirits of them have really much more of the temper of fairy physicians than of gnomes: each—as it were with sensitive hazel wand instead of smiting rod—beckoning, out of sparry caves, effervescent Brunnen, beneficently salt and warm.

24. At the very heart of this Enchanted chain, then—(and the beneficentest, if one use it and guide it rightly, of all the Brunnen there,) sprang the fountain of the earliest Frank race; "in the principality of Waldeck,"—you can trace their current to no farther source; there it rises out of the earth.

'Frankenberg' (Burg), on right bank of the Eder, nineteen miles north of Marburg, you may find marked clearly in the map No. 18 of Black's General Atlas, wherein the cluster of surrounding bewitched mountains, and the valley of Eder-stream, otherwise (as the village higher up the dell still calls itself) "Engel-Bach," "Angel Brook," joining that of the Fulda, just above Cassel, are also delineated in a way intelligible to attentive mortal eyes. I should be plagued with the names in trying a woodcut; but a few careful pen-strokes, or wriggles, of your own off-hand touching, would give you the concurrence of the actual sources of Weser in a comfortably extricated form, with the memorable towns on them, or just south of them, on the other slope of the watershed, towards Maine. Frankenberg and Waldeck on Eder, Fulda and Cassel on Fulda, Eisenach on Werra, who accentuates himself into Weser after taking Fulda for bride, as Tees the Greta, beyond Eisenach, under the Wartzburg, (of which you have heard as a castle employed on Christian mission and Bible Society purposes), town-streets below hard paved with basalt—name of it, Iron-ach, significant of Thuringian armouries in the old time,—it is active with mills for many things yet.

25. The rocks all the way from Rhine, thus far, are jets and spurts of basalt through irony sandstone, with a strip of coal or two northward, by the grace of God not worth digging for; at Frankenberg even a gold mine; also, by Heaven's mercy, poor of its ore; but wood and iron always to be had for the due trouble; and, of softer wealth above ground,—game, corn, fruit, flax, wine, wool, and hemp! Monastic care over all, in Fulda's and Walter's houses—which I find marked by a cross as built by some pious Walter, Knight of Meiningen on the Boden-wasser, Bottom

water, as of water having found its way well down at last: so " Boden-See," of Rhine well got down out of Via Mala.

26. And thus, having got your springs of Weser clear from the rock; and, as it were, gathered up the reins of your river, you can draw for yourself, easily enough, the course of its farther stream, flowing virtually straight north, to the North Sea. And mark it strongly on your sketched map of Europe, next to the border Vistula, leaving out Elbe yet for a time. For now, you may take the whole space between Weser and Vistula (north of the mountains), as wild barbarian (Saxon or Goth); but, piercing the source of the Franks at Waldeck, you will find them gradually, but swiftly, filling all the space between Weser and the mouths of Rhine, passing from mountain foam into calmer diffusion over the Netherland, where their straying forest and pastoral life has at last to embank itself into muddy agriculture, and in bleak-flying sea mist, forget the sunshine on its basalt crags.

27. Whereupon, *we* must also pause, to embank ourselves somewhat; and before other things, try what we can understand in this

name of Frank, concerning which Gibbon tells us, in his sweetest tones of satisfied moral serenity—"The love of liberty was the ruling passion of these Germans. They deserved, they assumed, they maintained, the honourable epithet of Franks, or Freemen." He does not, however, tell us in what language of the time—Chaucian, Sicambrian, Chamavian, or Cattian—'Frank' ever meant Free: nor can I find out myself what tongue of any time it first belongs to; but I doubt not that Miss Yonge ('History of Christian Names,' Articles on Frey and Frank) gives the true root, in what she calls the High German "Frang," Free *Lord*. Not by any means a Free *Commoner*, or anything of the sort! but a person whose nature and name implied the existence around him, and beneath, of a considerable number of other persons who were by no means 'Frang,' nor Frangs. His title is one of the proudest then maintainable;—ratified at last by the dignity of age added to that of valour, into the Seigneur, or Monseigneur, not even yet in the last cockney form of it, 'Mossoo,' wholly understood as a republican term!

28. So that, accurately thought of, the

quality of Frankness glances only with the flat side of it into any meaning of 'Libre,' but with all its cutting edge, determinedly, and to all time, it signifies Brave, strong, and honest, above other men.* The old woodland race were never in any wolfish sense 'free,' but in a most human sense

* Gibbon touches the facts more closely in a sentence of his 22nd chapter. "The independent warriors of Germany, *who considered truth as the noblest of their virtues*, and freedom as the most valuable of their possessions." He is speaking especially of the Frankish tribe of the Attuarii, against whom the Emperor Julian had to re-fortify the Rhine from Cleves to Basle: but the first letters of the Emperor Jovian, after Julian's death, "delegated the military command of *Gaul* and Illyrium (what a vast one it was, we shall see hereafter), to Malarich, a *brave and faithful* officer of the nation of the Franks;" and they remain the loyal allies of Rome in her last struggle with Alaric. Apparently for the sake only of an interesting variety of language,—and at all events without intimation of any causes of so great a change in the national character,—we find Mr. Gibbon in his next volume suddenly adopting the abusive epithets of Procopius, and calling the Franks "a light and perfidious nation" (vii. 251). The only traceable grounds for this unexpected description of them are that they refuse to be bribed either into friendship or activity, by Rome or Ravenna; and that in his invasion of Italy, the grandson of Clovis did not previously send exact warning of his proposed route, nor even entirely signify his intentions till he had secured the bridge of the Po at Pavia; afterwards declaring his mind with sufficient distinctness by "assaulting, almost at the same instant, the hostile camps of the Goths and Romans, who, instead of uniting their arms, fled with equal precipitation."

Frank, outspoken, meaning what they had said, and standing to it, when they had got it out. Quick and clear in word and act, fearless utterly and restless always;—but idly lawless, or weakly lavish, neither in deed nor word. Their frankness, if you read it as a scholar and a Christian, and not like a modern half-bred, half-brained infidel, knowing no tongue of all the world but in the slang of it, is really opposed, not to Servitude,—but to Shyness!* It is to this

---

* For detailed illustration of the word, see 'Val d'Arno,' Lecture VIII.; 'Fors Clavigera,' Letters XLVI. 231, LXXVII. 137; and Chaucer, 'Romaunt of Rose,' 1212— "Next *him*" (the knight sibbe to Arthur) "daunced dame Franchise;"—the English lines are quoted and commented on in the first lecture of 'Ariadne Florentina' (§ 26); I give the French here:—

> "Apres tous ceulx estoit Franchise
> Que ne fut ne brune ne bise.
> Ains fut comme la neige blanche
> *Courtoyse* estoit, *joyeuse*, et *franche*.
> Le nez avoit long et tretis,
> Yeulx vers, riants; sourcilz faitis;
> Les cheveulx eut très-blons et longs
> Simple fut comme les coulons
> Le cœur eut doulx et debonnaire.
> *Elle n'osait dire ne faire*
> *Nulle riens que faire ne deust.*"

And I hope my girl readers will never more confuse Franchise with 'Liberty.'

day the note of the sweetest and Frenchest of French character, that it makes simply perfect *Servants*. Unwearied in protective friendship, in meekly dextrous omnificence, in latent tutorship; the lovingly availablest of valets,—the mentally and personally bonniest of bonnes. But in no capacity shy of you! Though you be the Duke or Duchess of Montaltissimo, you will not find them abashed at your altitude. They will speak 'up' to you, when they have a mind.

29. Best of servants: best of *subjects*, also, when they have an equally frank King, or Count, or Capital, to lead them; of which we shall see proof enough in due time;—but, instantly, note this farther, that, whatever side-gleam of the thing they afterwards called Liberty may be meant by the Frank name, you must at once now, and always in future, guard yourself from confusing their Liberties with their Activities. What the temper of the army may be towards its chief, is *one* question —whether either chief or army can be kept six months quiet,—another, and a totally different one. That they must either be fighting somebody or going somewhere, else, their life

isn't worth living to them; the activity and mercurial flashing and flickering hither and thither, which in the soul of it is set neither on war nor rapine, but only on change of place, mood—tense, and tension;—which never needs to see its spurs in the dish, but has them always bright, and on, and would ever choose rather to ride fasting than sit feasting,—this childlike dread of being put in a corner, and continual want of something to do, is to be watched by us with wondering sympathy in all its sometimes splendid, but too often unlucky or disastrous consequences to the nation itself as well as to its neighbours.

30. And this activity, which we stolid beefeaters, before we had been taught by modern science that we were no better than baboons ourselves, were wont discourteously to liken to that of the livelier tribes of Monkey, did in fact so much impress the Hollanders, when first the irriguous Franks gave motion and current to their marshes, that the earliest heraldry in which we find the Frank power blazoned seems to be founded on a Dutch endeavour to give some distantly satirical presentment of it. "For," says a most

ingenious historian, Mons. André Favine,—
'Parisian, and Advocate in the High Court of
the French Parliament in the year 1620'—
"those people who bordered on the river Sala,
called 'Salts,' by the Allemaignes, were on
their descent into Dutch lands called by the
Romans "Franci Salici"—(whence 'Salique'
law to come, you observe) "and by abridgment
'Salii,' as if of the verb 'salire,' that is to say
'saulter,' to leap"—(and in future therefore—
duly also to dance—in an incomparable manner)
—"to be quicke and nimble of foot, to leap and
mount well, a quality most notably requisite for
such as dwell in watrie and marshy places;
So that while such of the French as dwelt on
the great course of the river" (Rhine) "were
called 'Nageurs,' Swimmers, they of the
marshes were called 'Saulteurs,' Leapers, so
that it was a nickname given to the French in
regard both of their natural disposition and
of their dwelling; as, yet to this day, their
enemies call them French Toades, (or Frogs,
more properly) from whence grew the fable
that their ancient Kings carried such creatures
in their Armes."

31. Without entering at present into debate

whether fable or not, you will easily remember the epithet 'Salian' of these fosse-leaping and river swimming folk, (so that, as aforesaid, all the length of Rhine must be refortified against them) — epithet however, it appears, in its origin delicately Saline, so that we may with good discretion, as we call our seasoned Mariners, '*old* Salts,' think of these more brightly sparkling Franks as ' Young Salts,'— but this equivocated presently by the Romans, with natural respect to their martial fire and 'elan,' into 'Salii'— exsultantes,*—such as

* Their first mischievous exsultation into Alsace being invited by the Romans themselves, (or at least by Constantius in his jealousy of Julian,)—with "presents and promises,— the hopes of spoil, and a perpetual grant of all the territories they were able to subdue." Gibbon, chap. xix. (3, 208). By any other historian than Gibbon, (who has really no fixed opinion on any character, or question, but, safe in the general truism that the worst men sometimes do right, and the best often do wrong, praises when he wants to round a sentence, and blames when he cannot otherwise edge one)— it might have startled us to be here told of the nation which "deserved, assumed, and maintained the *honourable* name of freemen," that "*these undisciplined robbers* treated as their natural enemies all the subjects of the empire who possessed any property which they were desirous of acquiring." The first campaign of Julian, which throws both Franks and Alemanni back across the Rhine, but grants the Salian Franks, under solemn oath, their established territory in the Netherlands, must be traced at another time.

their own armed priests of war: and by us now with some little farther, but slight equivocation, into useful meaning, to be thought of as here first Salient, as a beaked promontory, towards the France we know of; and evermore, in brilliant elasticities of temper, a salient or out-sallying nation; lending to us English presently—for this much of heraldry we may at once glance on to—their 'Leopard,' not as a spotted or blotted creature, but as an inevitably springing and pouncing one, for our own kingly and princely shields.

Thus much, of their 'Salian' epithet may be enough; but from the interpretation of the Frankish one we are still as far as ever, and must be content, in the meantime, to stay so, noting however two ideas afterwards entangled with the name, which are of much descriptive importance to us.

32. "The French poet in the first book of his Franciades" (says Mons. Favine; but what poet I know not, nor can enquire) "encounters" (in the sense of en-quarters, or depicts as a herald) "certain fables on the name of the French by the adoption and composure of two *Gaulish* words joyned

together, Phere-Encos which signifieth 'Beare-*Launce*,' (—Shake-Lance, we might perhaps venture to translate,) a lighter weapon than the Spear beginning here to quiver in the hand of its chivalry—and Fere-encos then passing swiftly on the tongue into Francos;" —a derivation not to be adopted, but the idea of the weapon most carefully,—together with this following—that "among the arms of the ancient French, over and beside the Launce, was the Battaile-Axe, which they called *Anchon*, and moreover, yet to this day, in many Provinces of France, it is termed an *Achon*, wherewith they served themselves in warre, by throwing it a farre off at joyning with the enemy, onely to discover the man and to cleave his shield. Because this *Achon* was darted with such violence, as it would cleave the Shield, and compell the Maister thereof to hold down his arm, and being so discovered, as naked or unarmed; it made way for the sooner surprizing of him. It seemeth, that this weapon was proper and particuler to the French Souldior, as well him on foote, as on horsebacke. For this cause they called it *Franciscus*. Francisca, *securis oblonga, quam Franci librabant in Hostes.* For the Horseman, beside his shield and Francisca (Armes common, as wee have said, to the Footman), had also the Lance, which being broken, and serving to no further effect, he laid hand on his Francisca, as we learn the use of that weapon in the Archbishop of Tours, his second book, and twenty-seventh chapter."

33. It is satisfactory to find how respectfully these lessons of the Archbishop of Tours were received by the French knights; and curious to see the preferred use of the Francisca by all the best of them—down, not only to Cœur de Lion's time, but even to the day of Poitiers. In the last wrestle of the battle at Poitiers gate, "Là, fit le Roy Jehan de sa main, merveilles d'armes, et tenoit une hache de guerre dont bien se deffendoit et combattoit, —si la quartre partie de ses gens luy eussent ressemblé, la journée eust été pour eux." Still more notably, in the episode of fight which Froissart stops to tell just before, between the Sire de Verclef, (on Severn) and the Picard squire Jean de Helennes: the Englishman, losing his sword, dismounts

to recover it, on which Helennes *casts* his own at him with such aim and force "qu'il acconsuit l'Anglois es cuisses, tellement que l'espée entra dedans et le cousit tout parmi, jusqu'au hans."

On this the knight rendering himself, the squire binds his wound, and nurses him, staying fifteen days 'pour l'amour de lui' at Chasteleraut, while his life was in danger; and afterwards carrying him in a litter all the way to his own chastel in Picardy. His ransom however is 6,000 nobles—I suppose about 25,000 pounds, of our present estimate; and you may set down for one of the fatallest signs that the days of chivalry are near their darkening, how "devint celuy Escuyer, Chevalier, pour le grand profit qu'il eut du Seigneur de Verclef."

I return gladly to the dawn of chivalry, when, every hour and year, men were becoming more gentle and more wise; while, even through their worst cruelty and error, native qualities of noblest cast may be seen asserting themselves for primal motive, and submitting themselves for future training.

34. We have hitherto got no farther in our

notion of a Salian Frank than a glimpse of his two principal weapons,—the shadow of him, however, begins to shape itself to us on the mist of the Brocken, bearing the lance light, passing into the javelin,—but the axe, his woodman's weapon, heavy;—for economical reasons, in scarcity of iron, preferablest of all weapons, giving the fullest swing and weight of blow with least quantity of actual metal, and roughest forging. Gibbon gives them also a 'weighty' sword, suspended from a 'broad' belt: but Gibbon's epithets are always gratis, and the belted sword, whatever its measure, was probably for the leaders only; the belt, itself of gold, the distinction of the Roman Counts, and doubtless adopted from them by the allied Frank leaders, afterwards taking the Pauline mythic meaning of the girdle of Truth —and so finally; the chief mark of Belted Knighthood.

35. The Shield, for all, was round, wielded like a Highlander's target:—armour, presumably, nothing but hard-tanned leather, or patiently close knitted hemp; "Their close apparel," says Mr. Gibbon, "accurately expressed the figure of their limbs," but 'apparel'

is only Miltonic-Gibbonian for 'nobody knows what.' He is more intelligible of their persons. "The lofty stature of the Franks, and their blue eyes, denoted a Germanic origin; the warlike barbarians were trained from their earliest youth to run, to leap, to swim, to dart the javelin and battle-axe with unerring aim, to advance without hesitation against a superior enemy, and to maintain either in life or death, the invincible reputation of their ancestors" (vi. 95). For the first time, in 358, appalled by the Emperor Julian's victory at Strasburg, and besieged by him upon the Meuse, a body of six hundred Franks "dispensed with the ancient law which commanded them to conquer or die." "Although they were strongly actuated by the allurements of rapine, they professed a disinterested love of war, which they considered as the supreme honour and felicity of human nature; and their minds and bodies were so hardened by perpetual action that, according to the lively expression of an orator, the snows of winter were as pleasant to them as the flowers of spring" (iii. 220).

36. These mental and bodily virtues, or

indurations, were probably universal in the military rank of the nation: but we learn presently, with surprise, of so remarkably 'free' a people, that nobody but the King and royal family might wear their hair to their own liking. The kings wore theirs in flowing ringlets on the back and shoulders, —the Queens, in tresses rippling to their feet,—but all the rest of the nation "were obliged, either by law or custom, to shave the hinder part of their head, to comb their short hair over their forehead, and to content themselves with the ornament of two small whiskers."

37. Moustaches,—Mr. Gibbon means, I imagine: and I take leave also to suppose that the nobles, and noble ladies, might wear such tress and ringlet as became them. But again, we receive unexpectedly embarrassing light on the democratic institutions of the Franks, in being told that " the various trades, the labours of agriculture, and the arts of hunting and fishing, were *exercised by servile* hands for the *emolument* of the Sovereign."

'Servile' and 'Emolument,' however, though at first they sound very dreadful and very wrong, are only Miltonic-Gibbonian expressions of the general fact that the Frankish Kings had ploughmen in their fields, employed weavers and smiths to make their robes and swords, hunted with huntsmen, hawked with falconers, and were in other respects tyrannical to the ordinary extent that an English Master of Hounds may be. "The mansion of the long-haired Kings was surrounded with convenient yards and stables for poultry and cattle; the garden was planted with useful vegetables; the magazines filled with corn and wine either for sale or consumption; and the whole administration conducted by the strictest rules of private economy."

38. I have collected these imperfect, and not always extremely consistent, notices of the aspect and temper of the Franks out of Mr. Gibbon's casual references to them during a period of more than two centuries,—and the last passage quoted, which he accompanies with the statement that "one hundred and sixty of these rural palaces were scattered through the provinces of their kingdom," without telling us what kingdom, or at what period, must I think be held descriptive of

the general manner and system of their monarchy after the victories of Clovis. But, from the first hour you hear of him, the Frank, closely considered, is always an extremely ingenious, well meaning, and industrious personage;—if eagerly acquisitive, also intelligently conservative and constructive; an element of order and crystalline edification, which is to consummate itself one day, in the aisles of Amiens; and things generally insuperable and impregnable, if the inhabitants of them had been as sound-hearted as their builders, for many a day beyond.

39. But for the present, we must retrace our ground a little; for indeed I have lately observed with compunction, in re-reading some of my books for revised issue, that if ever I promise, in one number or chapter, careful consideration of any particular point in the next, the next never *does* touch upon the promised point at all, but is sure to fix itself passionately on some antithetic, antipathic, or antipodic, point in the opposite hemisphere. This manner of conducting a treatise I find indeed extremely conducive to impartiality and largeness of view; but can conceive it

to be—to the general reader—not only disappointing, (if indeed I may flatter myself that I ever interest enough to disappoint), but even liable to confirm in his mind some of the fallacious and extremely absurd insinuations of adverse critics respecting my inconsistency, vacillation, and liability to be affected by changes of the weather in my principles or opinions. I purpose, therefore, in these historical sketches, at least to watch, and I hope partly to correct myself in this fault of promise breaking, and at whatever sacrifice of my variously fluent or re-fluent humour, to tell in each successive chapter in some measure what the reader justifiably expects to be told.

40. I left, merely glanced at, in my opening chapter, the story of the vase of Soissons. It may be found (and it is very nearly the only thing that *is* to be found respecting the personal life or character of the first Louis) in every cheap popular history of France; with cheap popular moralities engrafted thereon. Had I time to trace it to its first sources, perhaps it might take another aspect. But I give it as you may anywhere find it—asking

you only to consider whether — even as so read — it may not properly bear a somewhat different moral.

41. The story is, then, that after the battle of Soissons, in the division of Roman, or Gallic spoil, the King wished to have a beautifully wrought silver vase for—'himself,' I was going to write—and in my last chapter *did* mistakenly infer that he wanted it for his better self,—his Queen. But he wanted it for neither;—it was to restore to St. Remy, that it might remain among the consecrated treasures of Rheims. That is the first point on which the popular histories do not insist, and which one of his warriors, claiming equal division of treasure, chose also to ignore. The vase was asked by the King in addition to his own portion, and the Frank knights, while they rendered true obedience to their king as a leader, had not the smallest notion of allowing him what more recent kings call 'Royalties'—taxes on everything they touch. And one of these Frank knights or Counts—a little franker than the rest—and as incredulous of St. Remy's saintship as a Protestant Bishop, or Positivist Philosopher—took upon him to

dispute the King's and the Church's claim, in the manner, suppose, of a Liberal opposition in the House of Commons; and disputed it with such security of support by the public opinion of the fifth century, that—the King persisting in his request—the fearless soldier dashed the vase to pieces with his war-axe, exclaiming " Thou shalt have no more than thy portion by lot."

42. It is the first clear assertion of French 'Liberté, Fraternité and Egalité,' supported, then, as now, by the destruction, which is the only possible active operation of "free" personages, of the art they cannot produce.

The King did not continue the quarrel. Cowards will think that he paused in cowardice, and malicious persons, that he paused in malignity. He *did* pause in anger assuredly; but biding its time, which the anger of a strong man always can, and burn hotter for the waiting, which is one of the chief reasons for Christians being told not to let the sun go down upon it. Precept which Christians now-a-days are perfectly ready to obey, if it is somebody else who has been injured; and indeed, the difficulty in such cases is usually to get them to think of the injury even while the Sun rises on their wrath.*

43. The sequel is very shocking indeed—to modern sensibility. I give it in the, if not polished, at least delicately varnished, language of the Pictorial History.

"About a year afterwards, on reviewing his troops, he went to the man who had struck the vase, and *examining his arms, complained* that *they* were in bad condition!" (Italics mine) " and threw them" (What? shield and sword?) " on the ground. The soldier stooped to recover them; and at that moment the King struck him on the head with his battle-axe, crying, 'Thus didst thou to the vase at Soissons.'" The Moral modern historian proceeds to reflect that "this—as an evidence of the condition of the Franks, and of the ties by which they were united,—gives but the idea of a band of Robbers and their chief." Which is, indeed, so far as I can myself look into and decipher the nature of things, the Primary idea to be entertained respecting most of the kingly and military organizations in this

* Read Mr. Plimsoll's article on coal mines for instance.

world, down to our own day; and, (unless perchance it be the Afghans and Zulus who are stealing our lands in England—instead of we theirs, in their several countries.) But concerning the *manner* of this piece of military execution, I must for the present leave the reader to consider with himself, whether indeed it be less Kingly, or more savage, to strike an uncivil soldier on the head with one's own battle-axe, than, for instance, to strike a person like Sir Thomas More on the neck with an executioner's,—using for the mechanism, and as it were guillotine bar and rope to the blow —the manageable forms of National Law, and the gracefully twined intervention of a polite group of noblemen and bishops.

44. Far darker things have to be told of him than this, as his proud life draws towards the close,—things which, if any of us could see clear *through* darkness, you should be told in all the truth of them. But we never can know the truth of Sin; for its nature is to deceive alike on the one side the Sinner, on the other the Judge. Diabolic—betraying whether we yield to it, or condemn: Here is Gibbon's sneer—if you care for it; but I

gather first from the confused paragraphs which conduct to it, the sentences of praise, less niggard than the Sage of Lausanne usually grants to any hero who has confessed the influence of Christianity.

45. "Clovis, when he was no more than fifteen years of age, succeeded, by his father's death, to the command of the Salian tribe. The narrow limits of his kingdom were confined to the island of the Batavians, with the ancient dioceses of Tournay and Arras; and at the baptism of Clovis, the number of his warriors could not exceed five thousand. The kindred tribes of the Franks who had seated themselves along the Scheldt, the Meuse, the Moselle, and the Rhine, were governed by their independent kings, of the Merovingian race, the equals, the allies, and sometimes the enemies of the Salic Prince. When he first took the field he had neither gold nor silver in his coffers, nor wine and corn in his magazines; but he imitated the example of Cæsar, who in the same country had acquired wealth by the sword, and purchased soldiers with the fruits of conquest. The untamed spirit of the Barbarians was taught to acknowledge the

advantages of regular discipline. At the annual review of the month of March, their arms were diligently inspected; and when they traversed a peaceful territory they were prohibited from touching a blade of grass. The justice of Clovis was inexorable; and his careless or disobedient soldiers were punished with instant death. It would be superfluous to praise the valour of a Frank; but the valour of Clovis was directed by cool and consummate prudence. In all his transactions with mankind he calculated the weight of interest, of passion, and of opinion; and his measures were sometimes adapted to the sanguinary manners of the Germans, and sometimes moderated by the milder genius of Rome, and Christianity.

46. "But the savage conqueror of Gaul was incapable of examining the proofs of a religion, which depends on the laborious investigation of historic evidence, and speculative theology. He was still more incapable of feeling the mild influence of the Gospel, which persuades and purifies the heart of a genuine convert. His ambitious reign was a perpetual violation of moral and Christian duties: his hands were

stained with blood, in peace as well as in war; and, as soon as Clovis had dismissed a synod of the Gallican Church, he calmly assassinated *all* the princes of the Merovingian race."

47. It is too true; but rhetorically put, in the first place—for we ought to be told how many 'all' the princes were;—in the second place, we must note that, supposing Clovis had in any degree "searched the Scriptures" as presented to the Western world by St. Jerome, he was likely, as a soldier-king, to have thought more of the mission of Joshua * and Jehu than of the patience of Christ, whose sufferings he thought rather of avenging than imitating: and the question whether the other Kings of the Franks should either succeed him, or, in envy of his enlarged kingdom, attack and dethrone, was easily in his mind

---

* The likeness was afterwards taken up by legend, and the walls of Angoulême, after the battle of Poitiers, are said to have fallen at the sound of the trumpets of Clovis. "A miracle," says Gibbon, "which may be reduced to the supposition that some clerical engineer had secretly undermined the foundations of the rampart." I cannot too often warn my honest readers against the modern habit of "reducing" all history whatever to 'the supposition that' . . . etc., etc. The legend is of course the natural and easy expansion of a metaphor.

convertible from a personal danger into the chance of the return of the whole nation to idolatry. And, in the last place, his faith in the Divine protection of his cause had been shaken by his defeat before Arles by the Ostrogoths; and the Frank leopard had not so wholly changed his spots as to surrender to an enemy the opportunity of a first spring.

48. Finally, and beyond all these personal questions, the forms of cruelty and subtlety— the former, observe, arising much out of a scorn of pain which was a condition of honour in their women as well as men, are in these savage races all founded on their love of glory in war, which can only be understood by comparing what remains of the same temper in the higher castes of the North American Indians; and, before tracing in final clearness the actual events of the reign of Clovis to their end, the reader will do well to learn this list of the personages of the great Drama, taking to heart the meaning of the *name* of each, both in its probable effect on the mind of its bearer, and in its fateful expression of the course of their acts, and the consequences of it to future generations.

1. Clovis. Frank form, Hluodoveh. 'Glorious Holiness,' or consecration. Latin Chlodovisus, when baptized by St. Remy, softening afterwards through the centuries into Lhodovisus, Ludovicus, Louis.
2. Albofleda. 'White household fairy'? His youngest sister; married Theodoric (Theutreich, 'People's ruler'), the great King of the Ostrogoths.
3. Clotilde. Hlod-hilda. 'Glorious Battle-maid.' His wife. 'Hilda' first meaning Battle, pure; and then passing into Queen or Maid of Battle. Christianized to Ste Clotilde in France, and Ste Hilda of Whitby cliff.
3. Clotilde. His only daughter. Died for the Catholic faith, under Arian persecution.
4. Childebert. His eldest son by Clotilde, the first Frank King in Paris. 'Battle Splendour,' softening into Hildebert, and then Hildebrandt, as in the Nibelung.
5. Chlodomir. 'Glorious Fame.' His second son by Clotilde.

6. Clotaire. His youngest son by Clotilde; virtually the destroyer of his father's house. 'Glorious Warrior.'
7. Chlodowald. Youngest son of Chlodomir. 'Glorious Power,' afterwards 'St. Cloud.'

49. I will now follow straight, through their light and shadow, the course of Clovis' reign and deeds.

A.D. 481. Crowned, when he was only fifteen. Five years afterwards, he challenges, "in the spirit, and almost in the language of chivalry," the Roman governor Syagrius, holding the district of Rheims and Soissons. "Campum sibi præparari jussit—he commanded his antagonist to prepare him a battle field"—see Gibbon's note and reference, chap. xxxviii. The Benedictine abbey of Nogent was afterwards built on the field, marked by a circle of Pagan sepulchres. "Clovis bestowed the adjacent lands of Leuilly and Coucy on the church of Rheims." *

---

* When ?—for this tradition, as well as that of the vase, points to a friendship between Clovis and St. Remy, and a singular respect on the King's side for the Christians of Gaul, though he was not yet himself converted.

A.D. 485. The Battle of Soissons. Not dated by Gibbon: the subsequent death of Syagrius at the court of (the younger) Alaric, was in 486—take 485 for the battle.

50. A.D. 493. I cannot find any account of the relations between Clovis and the King of Burgundy, the uncle of Clotilde, which preceded his betrothal to the orphan princess. Her uncle, according to the common history, had killed both her father and mother, and compelled her sister to take the veil—motives none assigned, nor authorities. Clotilde herself was pursued on her way to France,* and

---

* It is a curious proof of the want in vulgar historians of the slightest sense of the vital interest of anything they tell, that neither in Gibbon, nor in Messrs. Bussey and Gaspey, nor in the elaborate 'Histoire des Villes de France,' can I find, with the best research my winter's morning allows, what city was at this time the capital of Burgundy, or at least in which of its four nominal capitals,—Dijon, Besancon, Geneva, and Vienne,—Clotilde was brought up. The evidence seems to me in favour of Vienne—(called always by Messrs. B. and G., 'Vienna,' with what effect on the minds of their dimly geographical readers I cannot say) —the rather that Clotilde's mother is said to have been "thrown into the *Rhone* with a stone round her neck." The author of the introduction to 'Bourgogne' in the 'Histoire des Villes' is so eager to get his little spiteful snarl at anything like religion anywhere, that he entirely forgets the existence of the first queen of France,—never names her, nor, as such, the place of her birth,—but contributes only

the litter in which she travelled captured, with part of her marriage portion. But the princess herself mounted on horseback, and rode, with part of her escort, forward into France, "ordering her attendants to set fire to everything that pertained to her uncle and his subjects which they might meet with on the way."

51. The fact is not chronicled, usually, among the sayings or doings of the Saints: but the punishment of Kings by destroying the property of their subjects, is too well recognized a method of modern Christian

to the knowledge of the young student this beneficial quota, that Gondeband, "plus politique que guerrier, trouva au milieu de ses controverses théologiques avec Avitus, évêque de *Vienne*, le temps de faire mourir ses trois frères et de recueillir leur heritage."

   The one broad fact which my own readers will find it well to remember is that Burgundy, at this time, by whatever king or victor tribe its inhabitants may be subdued, does practically include the whole of French Switzerland, and even of the German, as far east as Vindonissa :—the Reuss, from Vindonissa through Lucerne to the St. Gothard being its effective eastern boundary ; that westward—it meant all Jura, and the plains of the Säone ; and southward, included all Savoy and Dauphiné. According to the author of 'La Suisse Historique' Clotilde was first addressed by Clovis's herald disguised as a beggar, while she distributed alms at the gate of St. Pierre at Geneva ; and her departure and pursued flight into France were from Dijon.

warfare to allow our indignation to burn hot against Clotilde; driven, as she was, hard by grief and wrath. The years of her youth are not counted to us; Clovis was already twenty-seven, and for three years maintained the faith of his ancestral religion against all the influence of his queen.

52. A.D. 496. I did not in the opening chapter attach nearly enough importance to the battle of Tolbiac, thinking of it as merely compelling the Alemanni to recross the Rhine, and establishing the Frank power on its western bank. But infinitely wider results are indicated in the short sentence with which Gibbon closes his account of the battle. "After the conquest of the western provinces, the Franks *alone* retained their ancient possessions beyond the Rhine. They gradually subdued and *civilized* the exhausted countries as far as the Elbe and the mountains of Bohemia; and the *peace of Europe* was secured by the obedience of Germany."

53. For, in the south, Theodoric had already "sheathed the sword in the pride of victory and the vigour of his age—and his farther reign of three and thirty years was consecrated

to the duties of civil government." Even when his son-in-law, Alaric, fell by Clovis' hand in the battle of Poitiers, Theodoric was content to check the Frank power at Arles, without pursuing his success, and to protect his infant grandchild, correcting at the same time some abuses in the civil government of Spain. So that the healing sovereignty of the great Goth was established from Sicily to the Danube—and from Sirmium to the Atlantic ocean.

54. Thus, then, at the close of the fifth century, you have Europe divided simply by her watershed; and two Christian kings reigning, with entirely beneficent and healthy power—one in the north—one in the south—the mightiest and worthiest of them married to the other's youngest sister: a saint queen in the north—and a devoted and earnest Catholic woman, queen mother in the south. It is a conjunction of things memorable enough in the Earth's history,—much to be thought of, oh fast whirling reader, if ever, out of the crowd of pent up cattle driven across Rhine, or Adige, you can extricate yourself for an hour, to walk peacefully out of the south gate of Cologne, or across Fra Giocondo's bridge

at Verona—and so pausing look through the clear air across the battlefield of Tolbiac to the blue Drachenfels, or across the plain of St. Ambrogio to the mountains of Garda. For there were fought—if you will think closely—the two victor-battles of the Christian world. Constantine's only gave changed form and dying colour to the falling walls of Rome; but the Frank and Gothic races, thus conquering and thus ruled, founded the arts and established the laws which gave to all future Europe her joy, and her virtue. And it is lovely to see how, even thus early, the Feudal chivalry depended for its life on the nobleness of its womanhood. There was no *vision* seen, or alleged, at Tolbiac. The King prayed simply to the God of Clotilde. On the morning of the battle of Verona, Theodoric visited the tent of his mother and his sister, "and requested that on the most illustrious festival of his life, they would adorn him with the rich garments which they had worked with their own hands."

55. But over Clovis, there was extended yet another influence—greater than his queen's. When his kingdom was first extended to the Loire, the shepherdess of Nanterre was already

aged,—no torch-bearing maid of battle, like Clotilde, no knightly leader of deliverance like Jeanne, but grey in meekness of wisdom, and now "filling more and more with crystal light." Clovis's father had known her; he himself made her his friend, and when he left Paris on the campaign of Poitiers, vowed that if victorious, he would build a Christian church on the hills of Seine. He returned in victory, and with St. Genevieve at his side, stood on the site of the ruined Roman Thermæ, just above the "Isle" of Paris, to fulfil his vow: and to design the limits of the foundations of the first metropolitan church of Frankish Christendom.

The King "gave his battle-axe the swing," and tossed it with his full force.

Measuring with its flight also, the place of his own grave, and of Clotilde's, and St. Genevieve's.

There they rested, and rest,—in soul,— together. "La Colline tout entière porte encore le nom de la patronne de Paris; une petite rue obscure a gardé celui du Roi Conquerant."

III AMIENS.
Jour des Trepassés. 1880.

CHAPTER III.

THE LION TAMER.

1. IT has been often of late announced as a new discovery, that man is a creature of circumstances; and the fact has been pressed upon our notice, in the hope, which appears to some people so pleasing, of being able at last to resolve into a succession of splashes in mud, or whirlwinds in air, the 'circumstances' answerable for his creation. But the more important fact, that his nature is not levelled, like a mosquito's, to the mists of a marsh, nor reduced, like a mole's, beneath the crumblings of a burrow, but has been endowed with sense to discern, and instinct to adopt, the conditions which will make of it the best that can be, is very necessarily ignored by philosophers who propose, as a beautiful fulfilment of human destinies, a life entertained by scientific gossip, in a cellar lighted by electric sparks, warmed by tubular inflation,

drained by buried rivers, and fed, by the ministry of less learned and better provisioned races, with extract of beef, and potted crocodile.

2. From these chemically analytic conceptions of a Paradise in catacombs, undisturbed in its alkaline or acid virtues by the dread of Deity, or hope of futurity, I know not how far the modern reader may willingly withdraw himself for a little time, to hear of men who, in their darkest and most foolish day, sought by their labour to make the desert as the garden of the Lord, and by their love to become worthy of permission to live with Him for ever. It has nevertheless been only by such toil, and in such hope, that, hitherto, the happiness, skill, or virtue of man has been possible : and even on the verge of the new dispensation, and promised Canaan, rich in beatitudes of iron, steam, and fire, there are some of us, here and there, who may pause in filial piety to look back towards that wilderness of Sinai in which their fathers worshipped and died.

3. Admitting, however, for the moment, that the main streets of Manchester, the district

immediately surrounding the Bank in London, and the Bourse and Boulevards of Paris, are already part of the future kingdom of Heaven, when Earth shall be all Bourse and Boulevard, —the world of which our fathers tell us was divided to them, as you already know, partly by climates, partly by races, partly by times; and the 'circumstances' under which a man's soul was given to him, had to be considered under these three heads:—In what climate is he? Of what race? At what time?

He can only be what these conditions permit. With appeal to these, he is to be heard;—understood, if it may be;—judged, by our love, first—by our pity, if he need it— by our humility, finally and always.

4. To this end, it is needful evidently that we should have truthful maps of the world to begin with, and truthful maps of our own hearts to end with; neither of these maps being easily drawn at any time, and perhaps least of all now—when the use of a map is chiefly to exhibit hotels and railroads; and humility is held the disagreeablest and meanest of the Seven mortal Sins.

5. Thus, in the beginning of Sir Edward

Creasy's History of England, you find a map purporting to exhibit the possessions of the British Nation—illustrating the extremely wise and courteous behaviour of Mr. Fox to a Frenchman of Napoleon's suite, in "advancing to a terrestrial globe of unusual magnitude and distinctness, spreading his arms round it, over both the oceans and both the Indies," and observing, in this impressive attitude, that "while Englishmen live, they overspread the whole world, and clasp it in the circle of their power."

6. Fired by Mr. Fox's enthusiasm, the otherwise seldom fiery Sir Edward proceeds to tell us that "our island home is the favourite domicile of freedom, empire and glory," without troubling himself, or his readers, to consider how long the nations over whom our freedom is imperious, and in whose shame is our glory, may be satisfied in that arrangement of the globe and its affairs; or may be even at present convinced of their degraded position in it by his method of its delineation.

For, the map being drawn on Mercator's projection, represents therefore the British dominions in North America as twice the size of the States, and considerably larger than all South America put together: while the brilliant crimson with which all our landed property is coloured cannot but impress the innocent reader with the idea of a universal flush of freedom and glory throughout all those acres and latitudes. So that he is scarcely likely to cavil at results so marvellous by inquiring into the nature and completeness of our government at any particular place,—for instance in Ireland, in the Hebrides, or at the Cape.

7. In the closing chapter of the first volume of 'The Laws of Fésole' I have laid down the mathematical principles of rightly drawing maps;—principles which for many reasons it is well that my young readers should learn; the fundamental one being that you cannot flatten the skin of an orange without splitting it, and must not, if you draw countries on the unsplit skin, stretch them afterwards to fill the gaps.

The British pride of wealth which does not deny itself the magnificent convenience of penny Walter Scotts and penny Shakespeares, may assuredly, in its future greatness, possess itself also of penny universes, conveniently spinnable on their axes. I shall therefore assume that my readers can look at a round globe, while I am talking of the world; and at a properly reduced drawing of its surfaces, when I am talking of a country.

8. Which, if my reader can at present do— or at least refer to a fairly drawn double-circle map of the globe with converging meridians— I will pray him next to observe, that, although the old division of the world into four quarters is now nearly effaced by emigration and Atlantic cable, yet the great historic question about the globe is not how it is divided, here and there, by ins and outs of land or sea; but how it is divided into zones all round, by irresistible laws of light and air. It is often a matter of very minor interest to know whether a man is an American or African, a European or an Asiatic. But it is a matter of extreme and final interest to know if he be a Brazilian or a Patagonian, a Japanese or a Samoyede.

9. In the course of the last chapter, I asked the reader to hold firmly the conception of the great division of climate, which separated the

wandering races of Norway and Siberia from the calmly resident nations of Britain, Gaul, Germany, and Dacia.

Fasten now that division well home in your mind, by drawing, however rudely, the course of the two rivers, little thought of by common geographers, but of quite unspeakable importance in human history, the Vistula and the Dniester.

10. They rise within thirty miles of each other,* and each runs, not counting ins and outs, its clear three hundred miles, — the Vistula to the north-west, the Dniester to the south-east: the two of them together cut Europe straight across, at the broad neck of it,—and, more deeply looking at the thing, they divide Europe, properly so called—Europa's own, and Jove's—the small educationable, civilizable, and more or less mentally rational fragment of the globe, from the great Siberian wilderness, Cis-Ural and Trans-Ural; the inconceivable chaotic space, occupied datelessly by Scythians, Tartars, Huns, Cossacks, Bears, Ermines, and Mammoths, in various thickness of hide, frost of brain, and

* Taking the 'San' branch of Upper Vistula.

woe of abode—or of unabiding. Nobody's history worth making out, has anything to do with them; for the force of Scandinavia never came round by Finland at all, but always sailed or paddled itself across the Baltic, or down the rocky west coast; and the Siberian and Russian ice-pressure merely drives the really memorable races into greater concentration, and kneads them up in fiercer and more necessitous exploring masses. But by those exploring masses, of true European birth, our own history was fashioned for ever; and, therefore, these two truncating and guarding rivers are to be marked on your map of Europe with supreme clearness: the Vistula, with Warsaw astride of it half way down, and embouchure in Baltic,—the Dniester, in Euxine, flowing each of them, measured arrow straight, as far as from Edinburgh to London,—with windings,* the Vistula six hundred miles, and the Dniester five—count them together for a thousand miles of *moat*, between Europe and the Desert, reaching from Dantzic to Odessa.

* Note, however, generally that the strength of a river, cæteris paribus, is to be estimated by its straight course, windings being almost always caused by flats in which it can receive no tributaries.

11. Having got your Europe moated off into this manageable and comprehensible space, you are next to fix the limits which divide the four Gothic countries, Britain, Gaul, Germany, and Dacia, from the four classic countries, Spain, Italy, Greece, and Lydia.

There is no other generally opponent term to 'Gothic' but 'Classic': and I am content to use it for the sake of practical breadth and clearness, though its precise meaning for a little while remain unascertained. Only get the geography well into your mind, and the nomenclature will settle itself at its leisure.

12. Broadly, then, you have sea between Britain and Spain—Pyrenees between Gaul and Spain—Alps between Germany and Italy—Danube between Dacia and Greece. You must consider everything south of the Danube as Greek, variously influenced from Athens on one side, Byzantium on the other: then, across the Ægean, you have the great country absurdly called Asia Minor, (for we might just as well call Greece, Europe Minor, or Cornwall, England Minor,) but which is properly to be remembered as 'Lydia,' the country which infects with passion, and tempts with wealth; which

taught the Lydian measure in music, and softened the Greek language on its border into Ionic; which gave to ancient history the tale of Troy, and to Christian history, the glow, and the decline, of the Seven Churches.

13. Opposite to these four countries in the south, but separated from them either by sea or desert, are other four, as easily remembered —Morocco, Libya, Egypt, and Arabia.

Morocco, virtually consisting of the chain of Atlas and the coasts depending on it, may be most conveniently thought of as including the modern Morocco and Algeria, with the Canaries as a dependent group of islands.

Libya, in like manner, will include the modern Tunis and Tripoli: it will begin on the west with St. Augustine's town of Hippo; and its coast is colonized from Tyre and Greece, dividing it into the two districts of Carthage and Cyrene. Egypt, the country of the River, and Arabia, the country of *no* River, are to be thought of as the two great southern powers of separate Religion.

14. You have thus, easily and clearly memorable, twelve countries, distinct evermore by natural laws, and forming three zones from

north to south, all healthily habitable—but the races of the northern-most, disciplined in endurance of cold; those of the central zone, perfected by the enjoyable suns alike of summer and winter; those of the southern zone, trained to endurance of heat. Writing them now in tabular view,

Britain	Gaul	Germany	Dacia
Spain	Italy	Greece	Lydia
Morocco	Libya	Egypt	Arabia,

you have the ground of all useful profane history mapped out in the simplest terms; and then, as the fount of inspiration, for all these countries, with the strength which every soul that has possessed, has held sacred and supernatural, you have last to conceive perfectly the small hill district of the Holy Land, with Philistia and Syria on its flanks, both of them chastising forces: but Syria, in the beginning, herself the origin of the chosen race—"A Syrian ready to perish was my father"—and the Syrian Rachel being thought of always as the true mother of Israel.

15. And remember, in all future study of the relations of these countries, you must never allow your mind to be disturbed by the

accidental changes of political limit. No matter who rules a country, no matter what it is officially called, or how it is formally divided, eternal bars and doors are set to it by the mountains and seas, eternal laws enforced over it by the clouds and stars. The people that are born on it are *its* people, be they a thousand times again and again conquered, exiled, or captive. The stranger cannot be its king, the invader cannot be its possessor; and, although just laws, maintained whether by the people or their conquerors, have always the appointed good and strength of justice, nothing is permanently helpful to any race or condition of men but the spirit that is in their own hearts, kindled by the love of their native land.

16. Of course, in saying that the invader cannot be the possessor of any country, I speak only of invasion such as that by the Vandals of Libya, or by ourselves of India; where the conquering race does not become permanently inhabitant. You are not to call Libya Vandalia, nor India England, because these countries are temporarily under the rule of Vandals and English; neither Italy

Gothland under Ostrogoths, nor England Denmark under Canute. National character varies as it fades under invasion or in corruption; but if ever it glows again into a new life, that life must be tempered by the earth and sky of the country itself. Of the twelve names of countries now given in their order, only one will be changed as we advance in our history; —Gaul will properly become France when the Franks become her abiding inhabitants. The other eleven primary names will serve us to the end.

17. With a moment's more patience, therefore, glancing to the far East, we shall have laid the foundations of all our own needful geography. As the northern kingdoms are moated from the Scythian desert by the Vistula, so the southern are moated from the dynasties properly called 'Oriental' by the Euphrates; which, "partly sunk beneath the Persian Gulf, reaches from the shores of Beloochistan and Oman to the mountains of Armenia, and forms a huge hot-air funnel, the base" (or mouth) "of which is on the tropics, while its extremity reaches thirty-seven degrees of northern latitude. Hence it comes

that the Semoom itself (the specific and gaseous Semoom) pays occasional visits to Mosoul and Djezeerat Omer, while the thermometer at Bagdad attains in summer an elevation capable of staggering the belief of even an old Indian." *

18. This valley in ancient days formed the kingdom of Assyria, as the valley of the Nile formed that of Egypt. In the work now before us, we have nothing to do with its people, who were to the Jews merely a hostile power of captivity, inexorable as the clay of their walls, or the stone of their statues; and, after the birth of Christ, the marshy valley is no more than a field of battle between West and East. Beyond the great river,—Persia, India, and China, form the southern 'Oriens.' Persia is properly to be conceived as reaching from the Persian Gulf to the mountain chains which flank and feed the Indus; and is the true vital power of the East in the days of Marathon: but it has no influence on Christian history except through Arabia; while, of the northern

* Sir F. Palgrave, 'Arabia,' vol. ii., p. 155. I gratefully adopt in the next paragraph his division of Asiatic nations, p. 160.

Asiatic tribes, Mede, Bactrian, Parthian, and Scythian, changing into Turk and Tartar, we need take no heed until they invade us in our own historic territory.

19. Using therefore the terms 'Gothic' and 'Classic' for broad distinction of the northern and central zones of this our own territory, we may conveniently also use the word 'Arab'* for the whole southern zone. The influence of Egypt vanishes soon after the fourth century, while that of Arabia, powerful from the beginning, rises in the sixth into an empire whose end we have not seen.† And you may most rightly conceive the religious principle which is the base of that empire, by remembering, that while the Jews forfeited their prophetic power by taking up the profession

---

* Gibbon's fifty-sixth chapter begins with a sentence which may be taken as the epitome of the entire history we have to investigate : "The three great nations of the world, the Greeks, the Saracens, and the Franks, encountered each other on the theatre of Italy." I use the more general word, Goths, instead of Franks; and the more accurate word, Arab, for Saracen; but otherwise, the reader will observe that the division is the same as mine. Gibbon does not recognize the Roman people as a nation — but only the Roman power as an empire.

† Recent events have shown the force of these words. (Note on revision, May, 1885.)

of usury over the whole earth, the Arabs returned to the simplicity of prophecy in its beginning by the well of Hagar, and are not opponents to Christianity; but only to the faults or follies of Christians. They keep still their faith in the one God who spoke to Abraham their Father; and are His children in that simplicity, far more truly than the nominal Christians who lived, and live, only to dispute in vociferous council, or in frantic schism, the relations of the Father, the Son, and the Holy Ghost.

20. Trusting my reader then in future to retain in his mind without confusion the idea of the three zones, Gothic, Classic, and Arab, each divided into four countries, clearly recognizable through all ages of remote or recent history;—I must farther, at once, simplify for him the idea of the Roman *Empire*, (see note to last paragraph,) in the manner of its affecting them. Its nominal extent, temporary conquests, civil dissensions, or internal vices, are scarcely of any historical moment at all; the real Empire is effectual only as an exponent of just law, military order, and mechanical art, to untrained races, and as a translation of Greek thought

into less diffused and more tenable scheme for them. The Classic zone, from the beginning to the end of its visible authority, is composed of these two elements—Greek imagination, with Roman order: and the divisions or dislocations of the third and fourth century are merely the natural apparitions of their differences, when the political system which concealed them was tested by Christianity. It seems almost wholly lost sight of by ordinary historians, that in the wars of the last Romans with the Goths, the great Gothic captains were all Christians; and that the vigorous and naïve form which the dawning faith took in their minds is a more important subject of investigation, by far, than the inevitable wars which followed the retirement of Diocletian, or the confused schisms and crimes of the lascivious court of Constantine. I am compelled, however, to notice the terms in which the last arbitrary dissolutions of the empire took place, that they may illustrate, instead of confusing, the arrangement of the nations which I would fasten in your memory.

21. In the middle of the fourth century you have, politically, what Gibbon calls "the

final division of the *Eastern* and *Western Empires.*" This really means only that the Emperor Valentinian, yielding, though not without hesitation, to the feeling now confirmed in the legions that the Empire was too vast to be held by a single person, takes his brother for his colleague, and divides, not, truly speaking, their authority, but their attention, between the east and the west. To his brother Valens he assigns the extremely vague " Præfecture of the East, from the lower Danube to the confines of Persia," while for his own immediate government he reserves the "warlike præfectures of Illyricum, Italy, and Gaul, from the extremity of Greece to the Caledonian rampart, and from the rampart of Caledonia to the foot of Mount Atlas." That is to say, in less poetical cadence, (Gibbon had better have put his history into hexameters at once,) Valentinian kept under his own watch the whole of Roman Europe and Africa, and left Lydia and Caucasus to his brother. Lydia and Caucasus never did, and never could, form an Eastern Empire,—they were merely outside dependencies, useful for taxation in peace, dangerous by their multitudes in war. There never was, from the seventh century before Christ to the seventh after Christ, but *one* Roman Empire, which meant, the power over humanity of such men as Cincinnatus and Agricola; it expires as the race and temper of these expire; the nominal extent of it, or brilliancy at any moment, is no more than the reflection, farther or nearer upon the clouds, of the flames of an altar whose fuel was of noble souls. There is no true date for its division; there is none for its destruction. Whether Dacian Probus or Noric Odoacer be on the throne of it, the force of its living principle alone is to be watched—remaining, in arts, in laws, and in habits of thought, dominant still in Europe down to the twelfth century;— in language and example, dominant over all educated men to this hour.

22. But in the nominal division of it by Valentinian, let us note Gibbon's definition (I assume it to be his, not the Emperor's) of European Roman Empire into "Illyricum, Italy, and Gaul." I have already said you must hold everything south of the Danube for Greek. The two chief districts immediately

south of the stream are upper and lower Mœsia, consisting of the slope of the Thracian mountains northward to the river, with the plains between it and them. This district you must notice for its importance in forming the Mœso-Gothic alphabet, in which the "Greek is by far the principal element,"* giving sixteen letters out of the twenty-four. The Gothic invasion under the reign of Valens is the first that establishes a Teutonic nation within the frontier of the empire; but they only thereby bring themselves more directly under its spiritual power. Their bishop, Ulphilas, adopts this Mœsian alphabet, two-thirds Greek, for his translation of the Bible, and it is universally disseminated and perpetuated by that translation, until the extinction or absorption of the Gothic race.

23. South of the Thracian mountains you have Thrace herself, and the countries confusedly called Dalmatia and Illyria, forming the coast of the Adriatic, and reaching inwards and eastwards to the mountain watershed. I have never been able to form a clear notion myself of the real character of the people of

* Milman, 'Hist. of Christianity,' vol. iii. p. 36.

these districts, in any given period; but they are all to be massed together as northern Greek, having more or less of Greek blood and dialect according to their nearness to Greece proper; though neither sharing in her philosophy, nor submitting to her discipline. But it is of course far more accurate, in broad terms, to speak of these Illyrian, Mœsian, and Macedonian districts as all Greek, than with Gibbon or Valentinian to speak of Greece and Macedonia as all Illyrian.*

24. In the same imperial or poetical generalization, we find England massed with France under the term Gaul, and bounded by the "Caledonian rampart." Whereas in our own division, Caledonia, Hibernia, and Wales, are from the first considered as essential parts of Britain,† and the link with the continent is to

---

* I find the same generalization expressed to the modern student under the term 'Balkan Peninsula,' extinguishing every ray and trace of past history at once.

† Gibbon's more deliberate statement is clear enough. "From the coast or the extremity of Caithness and Ulster, the memory of Celtic origin was distinctly preserved in the perpetual resemblance of languages, religion, and manners, and the peculiar character of the British tribes might be naturally ascribed to the influence of accidental and local circumstances." The Lowland Scots, "wheat-eaters" or Wanderers, and the Irish, are very positively identified by

be conceived as formed by the settlement of Britons in Brittany, and not at all by Roman authority beyond the Humber.

25. Thus, then, once more reviewing our order of countries, and noting only that the British Islands, though for the most part thrown by measured degree much north of the rest of the north zone, are brought by the influence of the Gulf Stream into the same climate;—you have, at the time when our history of Christianity begins, the Gothic zone yet unconverted, and having not yet even heard of the new faith. You have the Classic zone variously and increasingly conscious of it, disputing with it, striving to extinguish it— and your Arab zone, the ground and sustenance of it, encompassing the Holy Land with the warmth of its own wings, and cherishing

---

Gibbon at the time our own history begins. "It is *certain*" (italics his, not mine) "that in the declining age of the Roman Empire, Caledonia, Ireland, and the Isle of Man, were inhabited by the Scots."—Chap. 25, vol. iv., p. 279.

The higher civilization and feebler courage of the Lowland *English* rendered them either the victims of Scotland, or the grateful subjects of Rome. The mountaineers, Pict among the Grampians, or of their own colour in Cornwall and Wales, have never been either instructed or subdued, and remain to this day the artless and fearless strength of the British race.

there—embers of phœnix fire over all the earth—the hope of Resurrection.

26. What would have been the course, or issue, of Christianity, had it been orally preached only, and unsupported by its poetical literature, might be the subject of deeply instructive speculation—if a historian's duty were to reflect instead of record. The power of the Christian faith was however, in the fact of it, always founded on the written prophecies and histories of the Bible; and on the interpretations of their meaning, given by the example, far more than by the precept, of the great monastic orders. The poetry and history of the Syrian Testaments were given to the Latin Church by St. Jerome, while the virtue and efficiency of monastic life are summed, in the rule of St. Benedict. To understand the relation of the work of these two men to the general order of the Church, is quite the first requirement for its farther intelligible history.

Gibbon's thirty-seventh chapter professes to give an account of the 'Institution of the Monastic Life' in the third century. But the monastic life had been instituted somewhat earlier, and by many prophets and kings. By

Jacob, when he laid the stone for his pillow; by Moses, when he drew aside to see the burning bush; by David, before he had left "those few sheep in the wilderness"; and by the prophet who "was in the deserts till the time of his showing unto Israel." Its primary "institution," for Europe, was Numa's, in that of the Vestal Virgins, and College of Augurs; founded on the originally Etrurian and derived Roman conception of pure life dedicate to the service of God, and practical wisdom dependent on His guidance.*

The form which the monastic spirit took in later times depended far more on the corruption of the common world, from which it was forced to recoil either in indignation or terror, than on any change brought about by Christianity in the ideal of human virtue and happiness.

27. "Egypt" (Mr. Gibbon thus begins to

---

* I should myself mark as the fatallest instant in the decline of the Roman Empire, Julian's rejection of the counsel of the Augurs. "For the last time, the Etruscan Haruspices accompanied a Roman Emperor, but by a singular fatality their adverse interpretation of the signs of heaven was disdained, and Julian followed the advice of the philosophers, who coloured their predictions with the bright hues of the Emperor's ambition." (Milman, 'Hist. of Christianity,' chap. vi.)

account for the new Institution!), "the fruitful parent of superstition, afforded the first example of monastic life." Egypt had her superstitions, like other countries; but was so little the *parent* of superstition that perhaps no faith among the imaginative races of the world has been so feebly missionary as hers. She never prevailed on even the nearest of her neighbours to worship cats or cobras with her; and I am alone, to my belief, among recent scholars, in maintaining Herodotus' statement of her influence on the archaic theology of Greece. But that influence, if any, was formative and delineative; not ritual: so that in no case, and in no country, was Egypt the parent of Superstition: while she was beyond all dispute, for all people and to all time, the parent of Geometry, Astronomy, Architecture, and Chivalry. She was, in its material and technic elements, the mistress of Literature, showing authors who before could only scratch on wax and wood, how to weave paper and engrave porphyry. She was the first exponent of the law of Judgment after Death for Sin. She was the Tutress of Moses; and the Hostess of Christ.

28. It is both probable and natural that, in such a country, the disciples of any new spiritual doctrine should bring it to closer trial than was possible among the illiterate warriors, or in the storm-vexed solitudes of the North; yet it is a thoughtless error to deduce the subsequent power of cloistered fraternity from the lonely passions of Egyptian monachism. The anchorites of the first three centuries vanish like feverish spectres, when the rational, merciful, and laborious laws of Christian societies are established; and the clearly recognizable rewards of heavenly solitude are granted to those only who seek the Desert for its redemption.*

29. 'The clearly *recognizable* rewards,' I repeat, and with cautious emphasis. No man has any data for estimating, far less right of judging, the results of a life of resolute self-denial, until he has had the courage to try it himself, at least for a time: but I believe no reasonable person will wish, and no honest person dare, to deny the benefits he has

* Even the best Catholic historians are too commonly blind to the inviolable connection of monastic virtue with the Benedictine law of agricultural labour. (Note on revision, 1885.)

occasionally felt both in mind and body, during periods of accidental privation from luxury, or exposure to danger. The extreme vanity of the modern Englishman in making a momentary Stylites of himself on the top of a Horn or an Aiguille, and his occasional confession of a charm in the solitude of the rocks, of which he modifies nevertheless the poignancy with his pocket newspaper, and from the prolongation of which he thankfully escapes to the nearest table-d'hôte, ought to make us less scornful of the pride, and more intelligent of the passion, in which the mountain anchorites of Arabia and Palestine condemned themselves to lives of seclusion and suffering, which were comforted only by supernatural vision, or celestial hope. That phases of mental disease are the necessary consequence of exaggerated and independent emotion of any kind must, of course, be remembered in reading the legends of the wilderness; but neither physicians nor moralists have yet attempted to distinguish the morbid states of intellect * which are extremities of noble

---

* Gibbon's hypothetical conclusion respecting the effects of self-mortification, and his following historical statement,

passion, from those which are the punishments of ambition, avarice, or lasciviousness.

30. Setting all questions of this nature aside for the moment, my younger readers need only hold the broad fact that during the whole of the fourth century, multitudes of self-devoted men led lives of extreme misery and poverty in the effort to obtain some closer knowledge of the Being and Will of God. We know, in any

---

must be noted as in themselves containing the entire views of the modern philosophies and policies which have since changed the monasteries of Italy into barracks, and the churches of France into magazines. "This voluntary martyrdom *must* have gradually destroyed the sensibility, both of mind and body; nor *can it be presumed* that the fanatics who torment themselves, are capable of any lively affection for the rest of mankind. *A cruel unfeeling temper has characterized the monks of every age and country.*"

How much of penetration, or judgment, this sentence exhibits, I hope will become manifest to the reader as I unfold before him the actual history of his faith; but being, I suppose, myself one of the last surviving witnesses of the character of recluse life as it still existed in the beginning of this century, I can point to the portraiture of it given by Scott in the introduction to 'The Monastery' as one perfect and trustworthy, to the letter and to the spirit; and for myself can say, that the most gentle, refined, and in the deepest sense amiable, phases of character I have ever known, have been either those of monks, or of domestic servants trained in the Catholic faith. (And, when I wrote this sentence—I did not know Miss Alexander's Edwige. Note on revision, 1885.)

available clearness, neither what they suffered, nor what they learned. We cannot estimate the solemnizing or reproving power of their examples on the less zealous Christian world; and only God knows how far their prayers for it were heard, or their persons accepted. This only we may observe with reverence, that among all their numbers, none seem to have repented their chosen manner of existence; none perish by melancholy or suicide; their self-adjudged sufferings are never inflicted in the hope of shortening the lives they embitter or purify; and the hours of dream or meditation, on mountain or in cave, appear seldom to have dragged so heavily as those which, without either vision or reflection, we pass ourselves, on the embankment and in the tunnel.

31. But whatever may be alleged, after ultimate and honest scrutiny, of the follies or virtues of anchorite life, we are unjust to Jerome if we think of him as its introducer into the West of Europe. He passed through it himself as a phase of spiritual discipline; but he represents, in his total nature and final work, not the vexed inactivity of the Eremite, but the eager industry of a benevolent tutor

and pastor. His heart is in continual fervour of admiration or of hope—remaining to the last as impetuous as a child's but as affectionate; and the discrepancies of Protestant objection by which his character has been confused, or concealed, may be gathered into some dim picture of his real self when once we comprehend the simplicity of his faith, and sympathise a little with the eager charity which can so easily be wounded into indignation, and is never repressed by policy.

32. The slight trust which can be placed in modern readings of him, as they now stand, may be at once proved by comparing the two passages in which Milman has variously guessed at the leading principles of his political conduct. "Jerome began (!) and ended his career as a monk of Palestine; he attained, *he aspired to*, no dignity in the Church. Though ordained a presbyter against his will, he escaped the episcopal dignity which was forced upon his distinguished contemporaries." ('History of Christianity,' Book III.)

"Jerome cherished the secret hope, if it was not the avowed object of his ambition, to succeed Damasus as Bishop of Rome. Is the rejection of an aspirant so singularly unfit for the station, from his violent passions, his insolent treatment of his adversaries, his utter want of self-command, his almost unrivalled faculty of awakening hatred, to be attributed to the sagacious and intuitive wisdom of Rome?" ('History of *Latin* Christianity,' Book I., chap. ii.)

33. You may observe, as an almost unexceptional character in the "sagacious wisdom" of the Protestant clerical mind, that it instinctively assumes *the desire of power and place not only to be universal* in Priesthood, but to be always *purely selfish* in the ground of it. The idea that power might possibly be desired for the sake of its benevolent use, so far as I remember, does not once occur in the pages of any ecclesiastical historian of recent date. In our own reading of past ages we will, with the reader's permission, very calmly put out of court all accounts of "hopes cherished in secret"; and pay very small attention to the reasons for mediæval conduct which appear logical to the rationalist, and probable to the politician.* We concern

---

* The habit of assuming, for the conduct of men of sense and feeling, motives intelligible to the foolish, and probable

ourselves only with what these singular and fantastic Christians of the past audibly said, and assuredly did.

34. Jerome's life by no means "began as a monk of Palestine." Dean Milman has not explained to us how any man's could; but Jerome's childhood, at any rate, was extremely other than recluse, or precociously religious. He was born of rich parents living on their own estate, the name of his native town in North Illyria, Stridon, perhaps now softened into Strigi, near Aquileja. In Venetian climate, at all events, and in sight of Alps and sea. He had a brother and sister, a kind grandfather, and a disagreeable private tutor, and was a youth still studying grammar at Julian's death in 363.

to the base, gains upon every vulgar historian, partly in the ease of it, partly in the pride; and it is horrible to contemplate the quantity of false witness against their neighbours which commonplace writers commit, in the mere rounding and enforcing of their shallow sentences. "Jerome admits, indeed, with *specious but doubtful humility*, the inferiority of the unordained monk to the ordained priest," says Dean Milman in his eleventh chapter, following up his gratuitous doubt of Jerome's humility with no less gratuitous asseveration of the ambition of his opponents. "The clergy, *no doubt*, had the sagacity to foresee the *dangerous* rival as to influence and authority, which was rising up in Christian society."

III. THE LION TAMER.

35. A youth of eighteen, and well begun in all institutes of the classic schools; but, so far from being a monk, not yet a Christian;—nor at all disposed towards the severer offices even of Roman life! or contemplating with aversion the splendours, either worldly or sacred, which shone on him in the college days spent in its Capital city.

For the "power and majesty of Paganism were still concentrated at Rome; the deities of the ancient faith found their last refuge in the capital of the empire. To the stranger, Rome still offered the appearance of a Pagan city. It contained one hundred and fifty-two temples, and one hundred and eighty smaller chapels or shrines, still sacred to their tutelary God, and used for public worship. Christianity had neither ventured to usurp those few buildings which might be converted to her use, still less had she the power to destroy them. The religious edifices were under the protection of the præfect of the city, and the præfect was usually a Pagan; at all events he would not permit any breach of the public peace, or violation of public property. Above all still towered the Capitol, in its unassailed and awful majesty, with its fifty temples or shrines, bearing the most sacred names in the religious and civil annals of Rome, those of Jove, of Mars, of Janus, of Romulus, of Cæsar, of Victory. Some years after the accession of Theodosius to the Eastern empire, the sacrifices were still performed as national rites at the public cost,—*the pontiffs made their offerings in the name of the whole human race.* The Pagan orator ventures to assert that the Emperor dared not to endanger the safety of the empire by their abolition. The Emperor still bore the title and insignia of the Supreme Pontiff; the Consuls, before they entered upon their functions, ascended the Capitol; the religious processions passed along the crowded streets, and the people thronged to the festivals and theatres which still formed part of the Pagan worship." *

36. Here, Jerome must have heard of what by all the Christian sects was held the judgment of God, between them and their chief enemy — the death of the Emperor Julian.

---

* Milman, 'History of Christianity,' vol. iii. p. 162. Note the sentence in italics, for it relates the true origin of the Papacy.

But I have no means of tracing, and will not conjecture, the course of his own thoughts, until the tenor of all his life was changed at his baptism. The candour which lies at the basis of his character has given us one sentence of his own, respecting that change, which is worth some volumes of ordinary confession. "I left, not only parents and kindred, but *the accustomed luxuries of delicate life.*" The words throw full light on what, to our less courageous temper, seems the exaggerated reading by the early converts of Christ's words to them—"He that loveth father or mother more than me, is not worthy of me." *We* are content to leave, for much lower interests, either father or mother, and do not see the necessity of any farther sacrifice: we should know more of ourselves and of Christianity if we oftener sustained what St. Jerome found the more searching trial. I find scattered indications of contempt among his biographers, because he could not resign one indulgence—that of scholarship; and the usual sneers at monkish ignorance and indolence are in his case transferred to the weakness of a pilgrim who was so luxurious as to carry his library in his wallet. It is a singular question (putting, as it is the modern fashion to do, the idea of Providence wholly aside), whether, but for the literary enthusiasm, which was partly a weakness, of this old man's character, the Bible would ever have become the library of Europe.

37. For that, observe, is the real meaning, in its first power, of the word *Bible*. Not book, merely; but 'Bibliotheca,' Treasury of Books: and it is, I repeat, a singular question, how far, if Jerome, at the very moment when Rome, his tutress, ceased from her material power, had not made her language the oracle of Hebrew prophecy, a literature of their own, and a religion unshadowed by the terrors of the Mosaic law, might have developed itself in the hearts of the Goth, the Frank, and the Saxon, under Theodoric, Clovis, and Alfred.

38. Fate had otherwise determined, and Jerome was so passive an instrument in her hands that he began the study of Hebrew as a discipline only, and without any conception of the task he was to fulfil, still less of the scope of its fulfilment. I could joyfully believe that the words of Christ, "If they

hear not Moses and the Prophets, neither will they be persuaded though one rose from the dead," had haunted the spirit of the recluse, until he resolved that the voice of Moses and the Prophets should be made audible to the Churches of all the earth. But so far as we have evidence, no such will or hope exalted the quiet instincts of his natural industry; partly as a scholar's exercise, partly as an old man's recreation, the severity of the Latin language was softened, like Venetian crystal, by the variable fire of Hebrew thought; and the "Book of Books" took the abiding form of which all the future art of the Western nations was to be an hourly enlarging interpretation.

39. And in this matter you have to note that the gist of it lies, not in the translation of the Hebrew and Greek Scriptures into an easier and a common language, but in their *presentation to the Church as of common authority*. The earlier Gentile Christians had naturally a tendency to carry out in various oral exaggeration or corruption, the teaching of the Apostle of the Gentiles, until their freedom from the bondage of the Jewish law

passed into doubt of its inspiration; and, after the fall of Jerusalem, even into horror-stricken interdiction of its observance. So that, only a few years after the remnant of exiled Jews in Pella had elected the Gentile Marcus for their Bishop, and obtained leave to return to the Ælia Capitolina built by Hadrian on Mount Zion, "it became a matter of doubt and controversy whether a man who sincerely acknowledged Jesus as the Messiah, but who still continued to observe the law of Moses, could possibly hope for salvation!"* While, on the other hand, the most learned and the most wealthy of the Christian name, under the generally recognised title of "knowing" (Gnostic), had more insidiously effaced the authority of the Evangelists by dividing themselves, during the course of the third century, "into more than fifty numerably distinct sects, and producing a multitude of histories, in which the actions and discourses of Christ and His Apostles were adapted to their several tenets."†

40. It would be a task of great, and in

* Gibbon, chap. xv. (II. 277).

† Ibid., II. 283. His expression "the most learned and most wealthy" should be remembered in confirmation of the evermore recurring fact of Christianity, that minds modest

nowise profitable difficulty to determine in what measure the consent of the general Church, and in what measure the act and authority of Jerome, contributed to fix in their ever since undisturbed harmony and majesty, the canons of Mosaic and Apostolic Scripture. All that the young reader need know is, that when Jerome died at Bethlehem, this great deed was virtually accomplished: and the series of historic and didactic books which form our present Bible, (including the Apocrypha) were established in and above the nascent thought of the noblest races of men living on the terrestrial globe, as a direct message to them from its Maker, containing whatever it was necessary for them to learn of His purposes towards them; and commanding, or advising, with divine authority and infallible wisdom, all that was best for them to do, and happiest to desire.

41. And it is only for those who have obeyed the law sincerely, to say how far the hope held out to them by the law-giver has been fulfilled. The worst "children of disobedience" are those who accept, of the Word,

in attainment, and lives careless of gain, are fittest for the reception of every constant Christian principle.

what they like, and refuse what they hate: nor is this perversity in them always conscious, for the greater part of the sins of the Church have been brought on it by enthusiasm which, in passionate contemplation and advocacy of parts of Scripture easily grasped, neglected the study, and at last betrayed the balance, of the rest. What forms and methods of self-will are concerned in the wresting of the Scriptures to a man's destruction, is for the keepers of consciences to examine, not for us. The history we have to learn must be wholly cleared of such debate, and the influence of the Bible watched exclusively on the persons who receive the Word with joy, and obey it in truth.

42. There has, however, been always a farther difficulty in examining the power of the Bible, than that of distinguishing honest from dishonest readers. The hold of Christianity on the souls of men must be examined, when we come to close dealing with it, under these three several heads: there is first, the power of the Cross itself, and of the theory of salvation, upon the heart,—then, the operation of the Jewish and Greek Scriptures on the

intellect,—then, the influence on morals of the teaching and example of the living hierarchy. And in the comparison of men as they are and as they might have been there are these three questions to be separately kept in mind,—first, what would have been the temper of Europe without the charity and labour meant by 'bearing the Cross'; then, secondly, what would the intellect of Europe have become without Biblical literature; and lastly, what would the social order of Europe have become without its hierarchy.

43. You see I have connected the words 'charity' and 'labour' under the general term of 'bearing the cross.' "If any man will come after me, let him deny himself, (for charity) and take up his cross (of pain) and follow me."

The idea has been *exactly* reversed by modern Protestantism, which sees, in the cross, not a furca to which it is to be nailed; but a raft on which it, and all its valuable properties,* are to be floated into Paradise.

* Quite one of the most curious colours of modern Evangelical thought is its pleasing connection of Gospel truth with the extension of lucrative commerce! See farther the note at p. 156.

44. Only, therefore, in days when the Cross was received with courage, the Scripture searched with honesty, and the Pastor heard in faith, can the pure word of God, and the bright sword of the Spirit, be recognised in the heart and hand of Christianity. The effect of Biblical poetry and legend on its intellect, must be traced farther, through decadent ages, and in unfenced fields;—producing 'Paradise Lost' for us, no less than the 'Divina Commedia';—Goethe's 'Faust,' and Byron's 'Cain,' no less than the 'Imitatio Christi.'

45. Much more, must the scholar, who would comprehend in any degree approaching to completeness, the influence of the Bible on mankind, be able to read the interpretations of it which rose into the great arts of Europe at their culmination. In every province of Christendom, according to the degree of art-power it possessed, a series of illustrations of the Bible were produced as time went on; beginning with vignetted illustrations of manuscript, advancing into life-size sculpture, and concluding in perfect power of realistic painting. These teachings and preachings of the Church,

by means of art, are not only a most important part of the general Apostolic Acts of Christianity; but their study is a necessary part of Biblical scholarship, so that no man can in any large sense understand the Bible itself until he has learned also to read these national commentaries upon it, and been made aware of their collective weight. The Protestant reader, who most imagines himself independent in his thought, and private in his study, of Scripture, is nevertheless usually at the mercy of the nearest preacher who has a pleasant voice and ingenious fancy; receiving from him thankfully, and often reverently, whatever interpretation of texts the agreeable voice or ready wit may recommend: while, in the meantime, he remains entirely ignorant of, and if left to his own will, invariably destroys as injurious, the deeply meditated interpretations of Scripture which, in their matter, have been sanctioned by the consent of all the Christian Church for a thousand years; and in their treatment, have been exalted by the trained skill and inspired imagination of the noblest souls ever enclosed in mortal clay.

46. There are few of the fathers of the

Christian Church whose commentaries on the Bible or personal theories of its gospel, have not been, to the constant exultation of the enemies of the Church, fretted and disgraced by angers of controversy, or weakened and distracted by irreconcilable heresy. On the contrary, the scriptural teaching, through their art, of such men as Orcagna, Giotto, Angelico, Luca della Robbia, and Luini, is, literally, free from all earthly taint of momentary passion; its patience, meekness, and quietness are incapable of error through either fear or anger; they are able, without offence, to say all that they wish; they are bound by tradition into a brotherhood which represents unperverted doctrines by unchanging scenes; and they are compelled by the nature of their work to a deliberation and order of method which result in the purest state and frankest use of all intellectual power.

47. I may at once, and without need of returning to this question, illustrate the difference in dignity and safety between the mental actions of literature and art, by referring to a passage, otherwise beautifully illustrative of St. Jerome's sweetness and simplicity

III. THE LION TAMER.

of character, though quoted, in the place where we find it, with no such favouring intention,—namely, in the pretty letter of Queen Sophie Charlotte (father's mother of Frederick the Great,) to the Jesuit Vota, given in part by Carlyle in his first volume, ch. iv.

"'How can St. Jerome, for example, be a key to Scripture?' she insinuates; citing from Jerome this remarkable avowal of his method of composing books;—especially of his method in that book, 'Commentary on the Galatians,' where he accuses both Peter and Paul of simulation, and even of hypocrisy. The great St. Augustine has been charging him with this sad fact, (says her Majesty, who gives chapter and verse,) and Jerome answers, 'I followed the commentaries of Origen, of'— five or six different persons, who turned out mostly to be heretics before Jerome had quite done with them, in coming years, 'And to confess the honest truth to you,' continues Jerome, 'I read all that, and after having crammed my head with a great many things, I sent for my amanuensis, and dictated to him, now my own thoughts, now those of others, without much recollecting the order, nor sometimes the words, nor even the sense'! In another place, (in the book itself further on *) he says, 'I do not myself write; I have an amanuensis, and I dictate to him what comes into my mouth. If I wish to reflect a little, or to say the thing better, or a better thing, he knits his brows, and the whole look of him tells me sufficiently that he cannot endure to wait.' Here is a sacred old gentleman whom it is not safe to depend upon for interpreting the Scriptures,—thinks her Majesty, but does not say so,—leaving Father Vota to his reflections." Alas, no, Queen Sophie, neither old St. Jerome's nor any other human lips nor mind, may be depended upon in that function; but only the Eternal Sophia, the Power of God and the Wisdom of God: yet this you may see of your old interpreter, that he is wholly open, innocent, and true, and that, through such a person, whether forgetful of his author, or hurried by his scribe, it is more than probable you may hear what Heaven knows to be best for you; and extremely improbable you should take the least harm, —while by a careful and cunning master in

* 'Commentary on the Galatians,' chap. iii.

the literary art, reticent of his doubts and dexterous in his sayings, any number of prejudices or errors might be proposed to you acceptably, or even fastened in you fatally, though all the while you were not the least required to confide in his inspiration.

48. For indeed, the only confidence, and the only safety which in such matters we can either hold or hope, are in our own desire to be rightly guided, and willingness to follow in simplicity the guidance granted. But all our conceptions and reasonings on the subject of inspiration have been disordered by our habit, first of distinguishing falsely—or at least needlessly—between inspiration of words and of acts; and secondly by our attribution of inspired strength or wisdom to some persons or some writers only, instead of to the whole body of believers, in so far as they are partakers of the Grace of Christ, the Love of God, and the Fellowship of the Holy Ghost. In the degree in which every Christian receives, or refuses, the several gifts expressed by that general benediction, he enters or is cast out from the inheritance of the saints,—in the exact degree in which he denies the Christ,

angers the Father, and grieves the Holy Spirit, he becomes uninspired or unholy,— and in the measure in which he trusts Christ, obeys the Father, and consents with the Spirit, he becomes inspired in feeling, act, word, and reception of word, according to the capacities of his nature. He is not gifted with higher ability, nor called into new offices, but enabled to use his granted natural powers, in their appointed place, to the best purpose. A child is inspired as a child, and a maiden as a maiden; the weak, even in their weakness, and the wise, only in their hour.

That is the simply determinable *theory* of the inspiration of all true members, of the Church; its truth can only be known by proving it in trial: but I believe there is no record of any man's having tried and declared it vain.*

* Compare the closing paragraph in p. 45 of 'The Shrine of the Slaves.' Strangely, as I revise *this* page for press, a slip is sent me from *The Christian* newspaper, in which the comment of the orthodox evangelical editor may be hereafter representative to us of the heresy of his sect; in its last audacity, actually *opposing* the power of the Spirit to the work of Christ. (I only wish I had been at Matlock, and heard the kind physician's sermon.)

"An interesting and somewhat unusual sight was seen in Derbyshire on Saturday last—two old-fashioned Friends, dressed in the original garb of the Quakers, preaching on

49. Beyond this theory of general inspiration, there is that of especial call and command, with actual dictation of the deeds to be done

the roadside to a large and attentive audience in Matlock. One of them, who is a doctor in good practice in the county, by name Dr. Charles A. Fox, made a powerful and effective appeal to his audience to see to it that each one was living in obedience to the light of the Holy Spirit within. Christ *within* was the hope of glory, and it was as He was followed in the ministry of the Spirit that we were saved by Him, who became thus to each the author and finisher of faith. He cautioned his hearers against building their house on the sand by believing in the free and easy Gospel so commonly preached to the wayside hearers, as if we were saved by 'believing' this or that. Nothing short of the work of the Holy Ghost in the soul of each one could save us, and to preach anything short of this was simply to delude the simple and unwary in the most terrible form.

"[*It would be unfair to criticise an address from so brief an abstract, but we must express our conviction that the obedience of Christ unto death, the death of the Cross, rather than the work of the Spirit in us, is the good tidings for sinful men.*—ED.]"

In juxtaposition with this editorial piece of modern British press theology, I will simply place the 4th, 6th, and 13th verses of Romans viii., italicising the expressions which are of deepest import, and always neglected. "That the *righteousness of the* LAW might be fulfilled *in us*, who walk not after the flesh, but after the Spirit. . . . For to be carnally *minded*, is death, but to be spiritually *minded*, is life, and peace. . . . For if ye live after the flesh, ye shall die; but if *ye through the Spirit* do mortify the *deeds* of the body, ye shall live."

It would be well for Christendom if the Baptismal service explained what it professes to abjure.

or words to be said. I will enter at present into no examination of the evidences of such separating influence; it is not claimed by the Fathers of the Church, either for themselves, or even for the entire body of the Sacred writers, but only ascribed to certain passages dictated at certain times for special needs: and there is no possibility of attaching the idea of infallible truth to any form of human language in which even these exceptional passages have been delivered to us. But this is demonstrably true of the entire volume of them, as we have it, and read,—each of us as it may be rendered in his native tongue; that, however mingled with mystery which we are not required to unravel, or difficulties which we should be insolent in desiring to solve, it contains plain teaching for men of every rank of soul and state in life, which so far as they honestly and implicitly obey, they will be happy and innocent to the utmost powers of their nature, and capable of victory over all adversities, whether of temptation or pain.

50. Indeed, the Psalter alone, which practically was the service book of the Church for

many ages, contains merely in the first half of it the sum of personal and social wisdom. The 1st, 8th, 12th, 14th, 15th, 19th, 23rd, and 24th psalms, well learned and believed, are enough for all personal guidance; the 48th, 72nd, and 75th, have in them the law and the prophecy of all righteous government; and every real triumph of natural science is anticipated in the 104th.

51. For the contents of the entire volume, consider what other group of historic and didactic literature has a range comparable with it. There are—

I. The stories of the Fall and of the Flood, the grandest human traditions founded on a true horror of sin.

II. The story of the Patriarchs, of which the effective truth is visible to this day in the polity of the Jewish and Arab races.

III. The story of Moses, with the results of that tradition in the moral law of all the civilized world.

IV. The story of the Kings—virtually that of all Kinghood, in David, and of all Philosophy, in Solomon : culminating in the Psalms and Proverbs, with the still more close and practical wisdom of Ecclesiasticus and the Son of Sirach.

V. The story of the Prophets—virtually that of the deepest mystery, tragedy, and permanent fate, of national existence.

VI. The story of Christ.

VII. The moral law of St. John, and his closing Apocalypse of its fulfilment.

Think, if you can match that table of contents in any other—I do not say 'book' but 'literature.' Think, so far as it is possible for any of us—either adversary or defender of the faith—to extricate his intelligence from the habit and the association of moral sentiment based upon the Bible, what literature could have taken its place, or fulfilled its function, though every library in the world had remained unravaged, and every teacher's truest words had been written down?

52. I am no despiser of profane literature. So far from it, that I believe no interpretations of Greek religion have ever been so affectionate, none of Roman religion so reverent, as those which will be found at the base of my art teaching, and current through the entire body of my works. But it was from the Bible that

I learned the symbols of Homer, and the faith of Horace: the duty enforced upon me in early youth of reading every word of the gospels and prophecies as if written by the hand of God, gave me the habit of awed attention which afterwards made many passages of the profane writers, frivolous to an irreligious reader, deeply grave to me. How far my mind has been paralysed by the faults and sorrow of life,—how far short its knowledge may be of what I might have known, had I more faithfully walked in the light I had, is beyond my conjecture or confession: but as I never wrote for my own pleasure or self-proclaiming, I have been guarded, as men who so write always will be, from errors dangerous to others; and the fragmentary expressions of feeling or statements of doctrine, which from time to time I have been able to give, will be found now by an attentive reader to bind themselves together into a general system of interpretation of Sacred literature,—both classic and Christian, which will enable him without injustice to sympathize in the faiths of candid and generous souls, of every age and every clime.

53. That there *is* a Sacred classic literature, running parallel with that of the Hebrews, and coalescing in the symbolic legends of mediæval Christendom, is shown in the most tender and impressive way by the independent, yet similar, influence of Virgil upon Dante, and upon Bishop Gawaine Douglas. At earlier dates, the teaching of every master trained in the Eastern schools was necessarily grafted on the wisdom of the Greek mythology; and thus the story of the Nemean Lion, with the aid of Athena in its conquest, is the real root-stock of the legend of St. Jerome's companion, conquered by the healing gentleness of the Spirit of Life.

54. I call it a legend only. Whether Heracles ever slew, or St. Jerome ever cherished, the wild or wounded creature, is of no moment to us in learning what the Greeks meant by their vase-outlines of the great contest, or the Christian painters by their fond insistance on the constancy of the Lion-friend. Former tradition, in the story of Samson,—of the disobedient Prophet,—of David's first inspired victory, and finally of the miracle wrought in the defence of the

most favoured and most faithful of the greater Prophets, runs always parallel in symbolism with the Dorian fable: but the legend of St. Jerome takes up the prophecy of the Millennium, and foretells, with the Cumæan Sibyl, and with Isaiah, a day when the Fear of Man shall be laid in benediction, not enmity, on inferior beings,—when they shall not hurt nor destroy in all the holy Mountain, and the Peace of the Earth shall be as far removed from its present sorrow, as the present gloriously animate universe from the nascent desert, whose deeps were the place of dragons, and its mountains, domes of fire.

Of that day knoweth no man; but the Kingdom of God is already come to those who have tamed in their own hearts what was rampant of the lower nature, and have learned to cherish what is lovely and human, in the wandering children of the clouds and fields.

AVALLON, 28*th August*, 1882.

CHAPTER IV.

INTERPRETATIONS.

1. IT is the admitted privilege of a custode who loves his cathedral to depreciate, in its comparison, all the other cathedrals of his country that resemble, and all the edifices on the globe that differ from it. But I love too many cathedrals—though I have never had the happiness of becoming the custode of even one—to permit myself the easy and faithful exercise of the privilege in question; and I must vindicate my candour, and my judgment, in the outset, by confessing that the cathedral of AMIENS has nothing to boast of in the way of towers,—that its central flèche is merely the pretty caprice of a village carpenter,—that the total structure is in dignity inferior to Chartres, in sublimity to Beauvais, in decorative splendour to Rheims, and in loveliness of figure-sculpture to Bourges. It has nothing like the artful pointing and moulding of the

arcades of Salisbury—nothing of the might of Durham;—no Dædalian inlaying like Florence, no glow of mythic fantasy like Verona. And yet, in all, and more than these, ways, outshone or overpowered, the cathedral of Amiens deserves the name given it by M. Viollet le Duc—

"The Parthenon of Gothic Architecture."*

2. Of Gothic, mind you; Gothic clear of Roman tradition, and of Arabian taint; Gothic pure, authoritative, unsurpassable, and unaccusable;—its proper principles of structure being once understood and admitted.

No well-educated traveller is now without some consciousness of the meaning of what is commonly and rightly called "purity of style," in the modes of art which have been practised by civilized nations; and few are unaware of the distinctive aims and character of Gothic. The purpose of a good Gothic builder was to raise, with the native stone of the place he had to build in, an edifice as high and as spacious as he could, with calculable and visible

---

* Of French Architecture, accurately, in the place quoted, "Dictionary of Architecture," vol. i., p. 71; but in the article "Cathédrale," it is called (vol. ii., p. 330) "l'église *ogivale* par excellence."

security, in no protracted and wearisome time, and with no monstrous or oppressive compulsion of human labour.

He did not wish to exhaust in the pride of a single city the energies of a generation, or the resources of a kingdom; he built for Amiens with the strength and the exchequer of Amiens; with chalk from the cliffs of the Somme,* and under the orders of two successive bishops, one of whom directed the foundations of the edifice, and the other gave thanks in it for its completion. His object, as a designer, in common with all the sacred builders of his time in the North, was to admit as much light into the building as was consistent with the comfort of it; to make its structure intelligibly

---

* It was a universal principle with the French builders of the great ages to use the stones of their quarries as they lay in the bed; if the beds were thick, the stones were used of their full thickness—if thin, of their necessary thinness, adjusting them with beautiful care to directions of thrust and weight. The natural blocks were never sawn, only squared into fitting, the whole native strength and crystallization of the stone being thus kept unflawed—"*ne dédoublant jamais* une pierre. Cette méthode est excellente, elle conserve à la pierre toute sa force naturelle,—tous ses moyens de resistance." See M. Viollet le Duc, Article "Construction" (Matériaux), vol. iv., p. 129. He adds the very notable fact that, *to this day, in seventy departments of France, the use of the stone-saw is unknown.*

admirable, but not curious or confusing; and to enrich and enforce the understood structure with ornament sufficient for its beauty, yet yielding to no wanton enthusiasm in expenditure, nor insolent in giddy or selfish ostentation of skill; and finally, to make the external sculpture of its walls and gates at once an alphabet and epitome of the religion, by the knowledge and inspiration of which an acceptable worship might be rendered, within those gates, to the Lord whose Fear was in His Holy Temple, and whose seat was in Heaven.

3. It is not easy for the citizen of the modern aggregate of bad building, and ill-living held in check by constables, which *we* call a town,—of which the widest streets are devoted by consent to the encouragement of vice, and the narrow ones to the concealment of misery, —not easy, I say, for the citizen of any such mean city to understand the feeling of a burgher of the Christian ages to his cathedral. For him, the quite simply and frankly-believed text, "Where two or three are gathered in my name, there am I in the midst of them," was expanded into the wider promise to many honest and industrious persons gathered in His name

—" They shall be my people and I will be their God";—deepened in his reading of it, by some lovely local and simply affectionate faith that Christ, as He was a Jew among Jews, and a Galilean among Galileans, was also, in His nearness to any—even the poorest —group of disciples, as one of their nation; and that their own " Beau Christ d'Amiens" was as true a compatriot to them as if He had been born of a Picard maiden.

4. It is to be remembered, however—and this is a theological point on which depended much of the structural development of the northern basilicas—that the part of the building in which the Divine presence was believed to be constant, as in the Jewish Holy of Holies, was only the enclosed choir; in front of which the aisles and transepts might become the King's Hall of Justice, as in the presence-chamber of Christ; and whose high altar was guarded always from the surrounding eastern aisles by a screen of the most finished workmanship; while from those surrounding aisles branched off a series of radiating chapels or cells, each dedicated to some separate saint. This conception of the company of Christ with

His saints, (the eastern chapel of all being the Virgin's,) was at the root of the entire disposition of the apse with its supporting and dividing buttresses and piers; and the architectural form can never be well delighted in, unless in some sympathy with the spiritual imagination out of which it rose. We talk foolishly and feebly of symbols and types: in old Christian architecture, every part is *literal:* the cathedral *is* for its builders the House of God;—it is surrounded, like an earthly king's, with minor lodgings for the servants; and the glorious carvings of the exterior walls and interior wood of the choir, which an English rector would almost instinctively think of as done for the glorification of the canons, was indeed the Amienois carpenter's way of making his Master-carpenter comfortable,*—nor less of showing his own

* The philosophic reader is quite welcome to 'detect' and 'expose' as many carnal motives as he pleases, besides the good ones,—competition with neighbour Beauvais—comfort to sleepy heads—solace to fat sides, and the like. He will find at last that no quantity of competition or comfort-seeking will do anything the like of this carving now;—still less his own philosophy, whatever its species: and that it was indeed the little mustard-seed of faith in the heart, with a very notable quantity of honesty besides in the habit and disposition, that made all the rest grow together for good.

native and insuperable virtue of carpenter, before God and man.

5. Whatever you wish to see, or are forced to leave unseen, at Amiens, if the overwhelming responsibilities of your existence, and the inevitable necessities of precipitate locomotion in their fulfilment, have left you so much as one quarter of an hour, not out of breath—for the contemplation of the capital of Picardy, give it wholly to the cathedral choir. Aisles and porches, lancet windows and roses, you can see elsewhere as well as here—but such carpenter's work, you cannot. It is late, —fully developed flamboyant just past the fifteenth century—and has some Flemish stolidity mixed with the playing French fire of it ; but wood-carving was the Picard's joy from his youth up, and, so far as I know, there is nothing else so beautiful cut out of the goodly trees of the world.

Sweet and young-grained wood it is : oak, *trained* and chosen for such work, sound now as four hundred years since. Under the carver's hand it seems to cut like clay, to fold like silk, to grow like living branches, to leap like living flame. Canopy crowning canopy, pinnacle piercing pinnacle — it shoots and wreathes itself into an enchanted glade, inextricable, imperishable, fuller of leafage than any forest, and fuller of story than any book.*

* Arnold Boulin, master-joiner (menuisier) at Amiens, solicited the enterprise, and obtained it in the first months of the year 1508. A contract was drawn and an agreement made with him for the construction of one hundred and twenty stalls with historical subjects, high backings, crownings, and pyramidal canopies. It was agreed that the principal executor should have seven sous of Tournay (a little less than the sou of France) a day, for himself and his apprentice, (threepence a day the two—say a shilling a week the master, and sixpence a week the man,) and for the superintendence of the whole work, twelve crowns a year, at the rate of twenty-four sous the crown; (*i.e.*, twelve shillings a year). The salary of the simple workman was only to be three sous a day. For the sculptures and histories of the seats, the bargain was made separately with Antoine Avernier, image-cutter, residing at Amiens, at the rate of thirty-two sous (sixteen pence) the piece. Most of the wood came from Clermont en Beauvoisis, near Amiens; the finest, for the bas-reliefs, from Holland, by St. Valery and Abbeville. The Chapter appointed four of its own members to superintend the work : Jean Dumas, Jean Fabres, Pierre Vuaille, and Jean Lenglaché, to whom my authors (canons both) attribute the choice of subjects, the placing of them, and the initiation of the workmen 'au sens véritable et plus élevé de la Bible ou des legendes, et portant quelque fois le simple savoir-faire de l'ouvrier jusqu'à la hauteur du génie du théologien.'

Without pretending to apportion the credit of savoir-faire and theology in the business, we have only to observe that the whole company, master, apprentices, workmen, image-

6. I have never been able to make up my mind which was really the best way of approaching the cathedral for the first time. If you have plenty of leisure, and the day is

cutter, and four canons, got well into traces, and set to work on the 3rd of July, 1508, in the great hall of the évêché, which was to be the workshop and studio during the whole time of the business. In the following year, another menuisier, Alexander Huet, was associated with the body, to carry on the stalls on the right hand of the choir, while Arnold Boulin went on with those on the left. Arnold, leaving his new associate in command for a time, went to Beauvais and St. Riquier, to see the woodwork there; and in July of 1511 both the masters went to Rouen together, 'pour étudier les chaires de la cathédrale.' The year before, also, two Franciscans, monks of Abbeville, 'expert and renowned in working in wood,' had been called by the Amiens chapter to give their opinion on things in progress, and had each twenty sous for his opinion, and travelling expenses.

In 1516, another and an important name appears on the accounts,—that of Jean Trupin, 'a simple workman at the wages of three sous a day,' but doubtless a good and spirited carver, whose true portrait it is without doubt, and by his own hand, that forms the elbow-rest of the 85th stall (right hand, nearest apse), beneath which is cut his name JHAN TRUPIN, and again under the 92nd stall, with the added wish, 'Jan Trupin, God take care of thee' (*Dieu te pourvoie*).

The entire work was ended on St. John's Day, 1522, without (so far as we hear) any manner of interruption by dissension, death, dishonesty, or incapacity, among its fellow-workmen, master or servant. And the accounts being audited by four members of the Chapter, it was found that the total expense was 9488 livres, 11 sous, and 3 obols

fine, and you are not afraid of an hour's walk, the really right thing to do is to walk down the main street of the old town, and

(décimes), or 474 napoleons, 11 sous, 3 décimes of modern French money, or roughly four hundred sterling English pounds.

For which sum, you perceive, a company of probably six or eight good workmen, old and young, had been kept merry and busy for fourteen years; and this that you see—left for substantial result and gift to you.

I have not examined the carvings so as to assign, with any decision, the several masters' work; but in general the flower and leaf design in the traceries will be by the two head menuisiers, and their apprentices; the elaborate Scripture histories by Avernier, with variously completing incidental grotesque by Trupin; and the joining and fitting by the common workmen. No nails are used,—all is morticed, and so beautifully that the joints have not moved to this day, and are still almost imperceptible. The four terminal pyramids 'you might take for giant pines forgotten for six centuries on the soil where the church was built; they might be looked on at first as a wild luxury of sculpture and hollow traceries—but examined in analysis they are marvels of order and system in construction, uniting all the lightness, strength, and grace of the most renowned spires in the last epoch of the Middle Ages.'

The above particulars are all extracted—or simply translated, out of the excellent description of the "Stalles et les Clôtures du Chœur" of the Cathedral of Amiens, by MM. les Chanoines Jourdain et Duval (Amiens, Vv. Alfred Caron, 1867). The accompanying lithographic outlines are exceedingly good, and the reader will find the entire series of subjects indicated with precision and brevity, both for the woodwork and the external veil of the choir, of which I have no room to speak in this traveller's summary.

across the river, and quite out to the chalk hill* out of which the citadel is half quarried —half walled;—and walk to the top of that, and look down into the citadel's dry 'ditch,' —or, more truly, dry valley of death, which is about as deep as a glen in Derbyshire, (or, more precisely, the upper part of the 'Happy Valley' at Oxford, above Lower Hincksey,) and thence across to the cathedral and ascending slopes of the city; so, you will understand the real height and relation of tower and town :—then, returning, find your way to the Mount Zion of it by any narrow cross streets and chance bridges you can— the more winding and dirty the streets, the better; and whether you come first on west front or apse, you will think them worth all the trouble you have had to reach them.

7. But if the day be dismal, as it may sometimes be, even in France, of late years, —or if you cannot or will not walk, which may also chance, for all our athletics and lawn-tennis,— or if you must really go to Paris this afternoon, and only mean to see all

---

* The strongest and finally to be defended part of the earliest city was on this height.

you can in an hour or two,—then, supposing that, notwithstanding these weaknesses, you are still a nice sort of person, for whom it is of some consequence which way you come at a pretty thing, or begin to look at it—I *think* the best way is to walk from the Hôtel de France or the Place de Perigord, up the Street of Three Pebbles, towards the railway station—stopping a little as you go, so as to get into a cheerful temper, and buying some bonbons or tarts for the children in one of the charming patissiers' shops on the left. Just past them, ask for the theatre; and just past that, you will find, also on the left, three open arches, through which you can turn, passing the Palais de Justice, and go straight up to the south transept, which has really something about it to please everybody. It is simple and severe at the bottom, and daintily traceried and pinnacled at the top, and yet seems all of a piece—though it isn't—and everybody *must* like the taper and transparent fretwork of the flèche above, which seems to bend to the west wind,—though it doesn't— at least, the bending is a long habit, gradually yielded into, with gaining grace and submissiveness, during the last three hundred years. And, coming quite up to the porch, everybody must like the pretty French Madonna in the middle of it, with her head a little aside, and her nimbus switched a little aside too, like a becoming bonnet. A Madonna in decadence she is, though, for all, or rather by reason of all, her prettiness, and her gay soubrette's smile; and she has no business there, neither, for this is St. Honoré's porch, not hers; and grim and grey St. Honoré used to stand there to receive you,—he is banished now to the north porch, where nobody ever goes in. This was done long ago, in the fourteenth-century days, when the people first began to find Christianity too serious, and devised a merrier faith for France, and would have bright-glancing, soubrette Madonnas everywhere—letting their own dark-eyed Joan of Arc be burnt for a witch. And thenceforward, things went their merry way, straight on, 'ça allait, ça ira,' to the merriest days of the guillotine.

But they could still carve, in the fourteenth century, and the Madonna and her hawthornblossom lintel are worth your looking at,—

much more the field above, of sculpture as delicate and more calm, which tells St. Honoré's own story, little talked of now in his Parisian faubourg.

8. I will not keep you just now to tell St. Honoré's story—(only too glad to leave you a little curious about it, if it were possible)*— for certainly you will be impatient to go into the church; and cannot enter it to better advantage than by this door. For all cathedrals of any mark have nearly the same effect when you enter at the west door; but I know no other which shows so much of its nobleness from the south interior transept; the opposite rose being of exquisite fineness in tracery, and lovely in lustre; and the shafts of the transept aisles forming wonderful groups with those of the choir and nave; also, the apse shows its height better, as it opens to you when you advance from the transept into the mid-nave, than when it is seen at once from the west end of the nave; where it is just possible for an irreverent person rather to think the nave narrow, than the apse high. Therefore,

---

* See, however, pages 32 and 130 (§§ 36, 112-114) of the octavo edition of 'The Two Paths.'

if you let me guide you, go in at this south
transept door, (and put a sou into every
beggar's box who asks it there,—it is none
of your business whether they should be there
or not, nor whether they deserve to have the
sou,—be sure only that you yourself deserve
to have it to give; and give it prettily, and
not as if it burnt your fingers). Then, being
once inside, take what first sensation and
general glimpse of it pleases you—promising
the custode to come back to *see* it properly;
(only then mind you keep the promise), and
in this first quarter of an hour, seeing only
what fancy bids you—but at least, as I said,
the apse from mid-nave, and all the traverses
of the building, from its centre. Then you
will know, when you go outside again, what
the architect was working for, and what his
buttresses and traceries mean. For the outside of a French cathedral, except for its
sculpture, is always to be thought of as the
wrong side of the stuff, in which you find how
the threads go that produce the inside or right-
side pattern. And if you have no wonder in
you for that choir and its encompassing circlet
of light, when you look up into it from the

cross-centre, you need not travel farther in search of cathedrals, for the waiting-room of any station is a better place for you;—but, if it amaze you and delight you at first, then, the more you know of it, the more it will amaze. For it is not possible for imagination and mathematics together, to do anything nobler or stronger than that procession of window, with material of glass and stone— nor anything which shall look loftier, with so temperate and prudent measure of actual loftiness.

9. From the pavement to the keystone of its vault is but 132 French feet—about 150 English. Think only—you who have been in Switzerland,—the Staubbach falls *nine* hundred! Nay, Dover cliff under the castle, just at the end of the Marine Parade, is twice as high; and the little cockneys parading to military polka on the asphalt below, think themselves about as tall as it, I suppose,— —nay, what with their little lodgings and stodgings and podgings about it, they have managed to make it look no bigger than a moderate-sized limekiln. Yet it is twice the height of Amiens' apse!—and it takes good

building, with only such bits of chalk as one can quarry beside Somme, to make your work stand half that height, for six hundred years.

10. It takes good building, I say, and you may even aver the best—that ever was, or is again likely for many a day to be, on the unquaking and fruitful earth, where one could calculate on a pillar's standing fast, once well set up; and where aisles of aspen, and orchards of apple, and clusters of vine, gave type of what might be most beautifully made sacred in the constancy of sculptured stone. From the unhewn block set on end in the Druid's Bethel, to *this* Lord's House and blue-vitrailed gate of Heaven, you have the entire course and consummation of the Northern Religious Builder's passion and art.

11. But, note further—and earnestly,—this apse of Amiens is not only the best, but the very *first* thing done *perfectly* in its manner, by Northern Christendom. In pages 323 and 327 of the sixth volume of M. Viollet le Duc, you will find the exact history of the development of these traceries through which the eastern light shines on you as you stand,

from the less perfect and tentative forms of Rheims: and so momentary was the culmination of the exact rightness, that here, from nave to transept—built only ten years later, —there is a little change, not towards decline, but to a not quite necessary precision. Where decline begins, one cannot, among the lovely fantasies that succeeded, exactly say — but exactly, and indisputably, we know that this apse of Amiens is the first virgin perfect work,—Parthenon also in that sense, — of Gothic Architecture.

12. Who built it, shall we ask? God, and Man, — is the first and most true answer. The stars in their courses built it, and the Nations. Greek Athena labours here—and Roman Father Jove, and Guardian Mars. The Gaul labours here, and the Frank: knightly Norman,—mighty Ostrogoth, — and wasted anchorite of Idumea.

The actual Man who built it scarcely cared to tell you he did so; nor do the historians brag of him. Any quantity of heraldries of knaves and fainéants you may find in what they call their 'history': but this is probably the first time you ever read the name of

Robert of Luzarches. I say he 'scarcely cared'—we are not sure that he cared at all. He signed his name nowhere, that I can hear of. You may perhaps find some recent initials cut by English remarkable visitors desirous of immortality, here and there about the edifice, but Robert the builder— or at least the Master of building, cut *his* on no stone of it. Only when, after his death, the headstone had been brought forth with shouting, Grace unto it, this following legend was written, recording all who had part or lot in the labour, within the middle of the labyrinth then inlaid in the pavement of the nave. You must read it trippingly on the tongue: it was rhymed gaily for you by pure French gaiety, not the least like that of the Théâtre de Folies.

> " En l'an de Grace mil deux cent
> Et vingt, fu l'œuvre de cheens
> Premièrement encomenchie.
> A donc y ert de cheste evesquie
> Evrart, évêque bénis ;
> Et, Roy de France, Loys
>   Qui fut fils Phelippe le Sage.
> Qui maistre y ert de l'œuvre
> Maistre Robert estoit només
> Et de Luzarches surnomés.

IV. INTERPRETATIONS. 183

> Maistre Thomas fu après lui
> De Cormont. Et après, son filz
> Maistre Regnault, qui mestre
> Fist a chest point chi cheste lectre
> Que l'incarnation valoit
> Treize cent, moins douze, en faloit."

13. I have written the numerals in letters, else the metre would not have come clear: they were really in figures thus, "II C. et XX," "XIII C. moins XII". I quote the inscription from M. l'Abbé Rozé's admirable little book, "Visite à la Cathédrale d'Amiens,"—Sup. Lib. de Mgr. l'Évêque d'Amiens, 1877,—which every grateful traveller should buy, for I'm only going to steal a little bit of it here and there. I only wish there had been a translation of the legend to steal, too; for there are one or two points, both of idea and chronology, in it, that I should have liked the Abbé's opinion of.

The main purport of the rhyme, however, we perceive to be, line for line, as follows:—

> "In the year of Grace, Twelve Hundred
> And twenty, the work, then falling to ruin,
> Was first begun again.
> Then was, of this Bishopric
> Everard the blessed Bishop.

> And, King of France, Louis,
> Who was son to Philip the Wise.
> He who was Master of the Work
> Was called Master Robert,
> And called, beyond that, of Luzarches.
> Master Thomas was after him,
> Of Cormont. And after him, his son,
> Master Reginald, who to be put
> Made—at this point—this reading.
> When the Incarnation was of account
> Thirteen hundred, less twelve, which it failed of."

In which legend, while you stand where once it was written (it was removed—to make the old pavement more polite—in the year, I sorrowfully observe, of my own earliest tour on the Continent, 1825, when I had not yet turned my attention to Ecclesiastical Architecture), these points are noticeable—if you have still a little patience.

14. 'The work'—*i.e.*, the Work of Amiens in especial, her cathedral, was 'déchéant,' falling to ruin, for the—I cannot at once say—fourth, fifth, or what time,—in the year 1220. For it was a wonderfully difficult matter for little Amiens to get this piece of business fairly done, so hard did the Devil pull against her. She built her first Bishop's church (scarcely more than St. Firmin's tomb-chapel) about the

year 350, just outside the railway station on the road to Paris ; * then, after being nearly herself destroyed, chapel and all, by the Frank invasion, having recovered, and converted her Franks, she built another and a properly called cathedral, where this one stands now, under Bishop St. Save, (St. Sauve, or Salve). But even this proper cathedral was only of wood, and the Normans burnt it in 881. Rebuilt, it stood for 200 years ; but was in great part destroyed by lightning in 1019. Rebuilt again, it and the town were more or less burnt together by lightning, in 1107,—my authority says calmly, "un incendie provoqué par la même cause détruisit *la ville*, et une partie de la cathédrale." The 'partie' being rebuilt once more, the whole was again reduced to ashes, "réduite en cendre par le feu de ciel en 1218, ainsi que tous les titres, les martyrologies, les calendriers, et les Archives de l'Evêché et du Chapitre."

15. It was the fifth cathedral, I count, then, that lay in 'ashes,' according to Mons. Gilbert —in ruin certainly—déchéant ;—and ruin of

---

* At St. Acheul. See the first chapter of this book, and the "Description Historique de la Cathédrale d'Amiens," by A. P. M. Gilbert, 8vo, Amiens, 1833, pp. 5-7.

a very discouraging completeness it would have been, to less lively townspeople—in 1218. But it was rather of a stimulating completeness to Bishop Everard and his people—the ground well cleared for them, as it were; and lightning (feu de l'enfer, not du ciel, recognized for a diabolic plague, as in Egypt), was to be defied to the pit. They only took two years, you see, to pull themselves together; and to work they went, in 1220, they, and their bishop, and their king, and their Robert of Luzarches. And this, that roofs you, was what their hands found to do with their might.

16. Their king was 'à-donc,' 'at that time,' Louis VIII., who is especially further called the son of Philip of August, or Philip the Wise, because his father was not dead in 1220; but must have resigned the practical kingdom to his son, as his own father had done to him; the old and wise king retiring to his chamber, and thence silently guiding his son's hands, very gloriously, yet for three years.

But, farther—and this is the point on which chiefly I would have desired the Abbé's judgment—Louis VIII. died of fever at Montpensier in 1226. And the entire conduct of the main labour of the cathedral, and the chief glory of its service, as we shall hear presently, was *Saint* Louis's; for a time of forty-four years. And the inscription was put "à ce point ci" by the last architect, six years after St. Louis's death. How is it that the great and holy king is not named?

17. I must not, in this traveller's brief, lose time in conjectural answers to the questions which every step here will raise from the ravaged shrine. But this is a very solemn one; and must be kept in our hearts, till we may perhaps get clue to it. One thing only we are sure of,—that at least the *due* honour —alike by the sons of Kings and sons of Craftsmen—is given always to their fathers; and that apparently the chief honour of all is given here to Philip the Wise. From whose house, not of parliament but of peace, came, in the years when this temple was first in building, an edict indeed of peace-making: "That it should be criminal for any man to take vengeance for an insult or injury till forty days after the commission of the offence—and

then only with the approbation of the Bishop of the Diocese." Which was perhaps a wiser effort to end the Feudal system in its Saxon sense,* than any of our recent projects for ending it in the Norman one.

18. "A ce point ci." The point, namely, of the labyrinth inlaid in the cathedral floor; a recognized emblem of many things to the people, who knew that the ground they stood on was holy, as the roof over their head. Chiefly, to them, it was an emblem of noble human life— strait-gated, narrow-walled, with infinite darknesses and the "inextricabilis error" on either hand—and in the depth of it, the brutal nature to be conquered.

19. This meaning, from the proudest heroic, and purest legislative, days of Greece, the symbol had borne for all men skilled in her traditions: to the schools of craftsmen the sign meant further their craft's noblesse, and pure descent from the divinely-terrestrial skill of Dædalus, the labyrinth-builder, and the first

---

* Feud, Saxon faedh, low Latin Faida (Scottish 'fae,' English 'foe,' derivative), Johnson. Remember also that the root of Feud, in its Norman sense of land-allotment, is *foi*, not *fee*, which Johnson, old Tory as he was, did not observe—neither in general does the modern Antifeudalist.

sculptor of imagery *pathetic** with human life and death.

20. Quite the most beautiful sign of the power of true Christian-Catholic faith is this continual acknowledgment by it of the brotherhood—nay, more, the fatherhood, of the elder nations who had not seen Christ; but had been filled with the Spirit of God; and obeyed, according to their knowledge, His unwritten law. The pure charity and humility of this temper are seen in all Christian art, according to its strength and purity of race; but best, to the full, seen and interpreted by the three great Christian-Heathen poets, Dante, Douglas of Dunkeld,† and George Chapman. The prayer with which the last ends his life's work is, so far as I know, the perfectest and deepest expression of Natural Religion given us in literature; and if you can, pray it here —standing on the spot where the builder

---

* "Tu quoque, magnam
Partem opere in tanto, sineret dolor, Icare, haberes,
Bis conatus erat casus effingere in auro,—
Bis patriæ cecidere manus."

There is, advisedly, no pathos allowed in primary sculpture. Its heroes conquer without exultation, and die without sorrow.

† See 'Fors Clavigera,' Letter LXI., p. 22.

once wrote the history of the Parthenon of Christianity.

21. "I pray thee, Lord, the Father, and the Guide of our reason, that we may remember the nobleness with which Thou hast adorned us; and that Thou would'st be always on our right hand and on our left,* in the motion of our own Wills: that so we may be purged from the contagion of the Body and the Affections of the Brute, and overcome them and rule; and use, as it becomes men to use them, for instruments. And then, that Thou would'st be in Fellowship with us for the careful correction of our reason, and for its conjunction by the light of truth with the things that truly are.

"And in the third place, I pray to Thee the Saviour, that thou would'st utterly cleanse away the closing gloom from the eyes of our souls, that we may know well who is to be held for God, and who for Mortal. Amen."†

---

* Thus, the command to the children of Israel "that they go forward" is to their own wills. They obeying, the sea retreats, *but not before* they dare to advance into it. *Then*, the waters are a wall unto them, on their right hand and their left.

† The original is written in Latin only. "Supplico tibi, Domine, Pater et Dux rationis nostræ, ut nostræ Nobilitatis recordemur, quâ tu nos ornasti: et ut tu nobis presto sis, ut

22. And having prayed this prayer, or at least, read it with honest wishing, (which if you cannot, there is no hope of your at present taking pleasure in any human work of large faculty, whether poetry, painting, or sculpture,) we may walk a little farther westwards down the nave, where, in the middle of it, but only a few yards from its end, two flat stones (the custode will show you them), one a little farther back than the other, are laid over the graves of the two great bishops, all whose strength of life was given, with the builder's, to raise this temple. Their actual graves have not been disturbed; but the tombs raised over them, once and again removed, are now set on your right and left hand as you look back to the apse, under the third arch between the nave and aisles.

23. Both are of bronze, cast at one flow—

iis qui per sese moventur; ut et a Corporis contagio, Brutorumque affectuum repurgemur, eosque superemus, atque regamus; et, sicut decet, pro instrumentis iis utamur. Deinde, ut nobis adjuncto sis; ad accuratam rationis nostræ correctionem, et conjunctionem cum iis qui verè sunt, per lucem veritatis. Et tertium, Salvatori supplex oro, ut ab oculis animorum nostrorum caliginem prorsus abstergas; ut norimus bene, qui Deus, aut Mortalis habendus. Amen."

and with insuperable, in some respects inimitable, skill in the caster's art.

"Chef-d'œuvres de fonte,—le tout fondu d'un seul jet, et admirablement."* There are only two other such tombs left in France, those of the children of St. Louis. All others of their kind—and they were many in every great cathedral of France—were first torn from the graves they covered, to destroy the memory of France's dead; and then melted down into sous and centimes, to buy gunpowder and absinthe with for her living,—by the Progressive Mind of Civilization in her first blaze of enthusiasm and new light, from 1789 to 1800.

The children's tombs, one on each side of the altar of St. Denis, are much smaller than these, though wrought more beautifully. These beside you are the *only two Bronze tombs of her Men of the great ages*, left in France!

24. And they are the tombs of the pastors

---

* Viollet le Duc, vol. viii., p. 256. He adds: "L'une d'elles est comme art" (meaning general art of sculpture), "un monument du premier ordre;" but this is only partially true —also I find a note in M. Gilbert's account of them, p. 126: "Les deux doigts qui manquent, à la main droite de l'évêque Gaudefroi paraissent être un défaut survenu à la fonte." See further, on these monuments, and those of St. Louis's children, Viollet le Duc, vol. ix., pp. 61, 62.

of her people, who built for her the first perfect temple to her God. The Bishop Everard's is on your right, and has engraved round the border of it this inscription : *—

"Who fed the people, who laid the foundations of this Structure, to whose care the City was given,
Here, in ever-breathing balm of fame, rests Everard.
A man compassionate to the afflicted, the widow's protector, the orphan's
Guardian. Whom he could, he recreated with gifts. To words of men,
If gentle, a lamb ; if violent, a lion ; if proud, biting steel."

English, at its best, in Elizabethan days, is a nobler language than ever Latin was; but its virtue is in colour and tone, not in what may be called metallic or crystalline

---

* I steal again from the Abbé Rozé the two inscriptions,— with his introductory notice of the evilly-inspired interference with them.

"La tombe d'Evrard de Fouilloy, (died 1222), coulée en bronze en plein-relief, était supportée, dès le principe, par des monstres engagés dans une maçonnerie remplissant le dessous du monument, pour indiquer que cet évêque avait posé les fondements de la Cathédrale. Un *architecte malheureusement inspiré* a osé arracher la maçonnerie, pour qu'on ne vit plus la main du prélat fondateur, à la base de l'édifice.

"On lit, sur la bordure, l'inscription suivante en beaux caractères du XIIIº siècle :

condensation. And it is impossible to translate the last line of this inscription in as few English words. Note in it first that the Bishop's friends and enemies are spoken of as in word, not act; because the swelling, or mocking, or flattering, words of men are indeed what the meek of the earth must know how to bear and to welcome;—their deeds, it is for kings and

> "'Qui populum pavit, qui fundamēta locavit
> Huiūs structure, cuius fuit urbs data cure
> Hic redolens nardus, famâ requiescit Ewardus,
> Vir pius ahflictis, vidvis tutela, relictis
> Custos, quos poterat recreabat munere ; vbis,
> Mitiß agnus erat, tumidis leo, lima supbis.'

"Geoffroy d'Eu (died 1237) est représenté comme son prédécesseur en habits épiscopaux, mais le dessous du bronze supporté par des chimères est évidé, ce prélat ayant élevé l'édifice jusqu'aux voûtes. Voici la légende gravée sur la bordure :

> "'Ecce premunt humile Gaufridi membra cubile.
> Seu minus aut simile nobis parat omnibus ille ;
> Quem laurus gemina decoraverat, in medicinâ
> Lege qū divina, decuerunt cornua bina ;
> Clare vir Augensis, quo sedes Ambianensis
> Crevit in imensis ; in coelis auctus, Amen, sis.'

Tout est à étudier dans ces deux monuments : tout y est d'un haut intérêt, quant au dessin, à la sculpture, à l'agencement des ornements et des draperies."

In saying above that Geoffroy of Eu returned thanks in the Cathedral for its completion, I meant only that he had brought at least the choir into condition for service: "Jusqu'aux voûtes" may or may not mean that the vaulting was closed.

knights to deal with: not but that the Bishops often took deeds in hand also; and in actual battle they were permitted to strike with the mace, but not with sword or lance—*i.e.*, not to "shed blood"! For it was supposed that a man might always recover from a mace-blow; (which, however, would much depend on the bishop's mind who gave it). The battle of Bouvines, quite one of the most important in mediæval history, was won against the English, and against odds besides of Germans, under their Emperor Otho, by two French bishops (Senlis and Bayeux) — who both generalled the French King's line, and led its charges. Our Earl of Salisbury surrendered to the Bishop of Bayeux in person.

25. Note farther, that quite one of the deadliest and most diabolic powers of evil words, or, rightly so called, blasphemy, has been developed in modern days in the effect of sometimes quite innocently meant and enjoyed 'slang.' There are two kinds of slang, in the essence of it: one 'Thieves' Latin '— the special language of rascals, used for concealment; the other, one might perhaps best call Louts' Latin!—the lowering or insulting

words invented by vile persons to bring good things, in their own estimates, to their own level, or beneath it. The really worst power of this kind of blasphemy is in its often making it impossible to use plain words without a degrading or ludicrous attached sense: —thus I could not end my translation of this epitaph, as the old Latinist could, with the exactly accurate image: "to the proud, a file" —because of the abuse of the word in lower English, retaining, however, quite shrewdly, the thirteenth-century idea. But the *exact* force of the symbol here is in its allusion to jewellers' work, filing down facets. A proud man is often also a precious one: and may be made brighter in surface, and the purity of his inner self shown, by good *filing*.

26. Take it all in all, the perfect duty of a Bishop is expressed in these six Latin lines, —au mieux mieux—beginning with his pastoral office—*Feed* my sheep—qui *pavit* populum. And be assured, good reader, these ages never could have told you what a Bishop's, or any other man's, duty was, unless they had each man in his place both done it well—and seen

it well done. The Bishop Geoffroy's tomb is on your left, and its inscription is:

"Behold, the limbs of Godfrey press their lowly bed,
   Whether He is preparing for us all one less than, or like it.
Whom the twin laurels adorned, in medicine
And in divine law, the dual crests became him.
Bright-shining man of Eu, by whom the throne of Amiens
Rose into immensity, be *thou* increased in Heaven."
                                                        Amen.

And now at last—this reverence done and thanks paid—we will turn from these tombs, and go out at one of the western doors—and so see gradually rising above us the immensity of the three porches, and of the thoughts engraved in them.

27. What disgrace or change has come upon them, I will not tell you to-day—except only the 'immeasurable' loss of the great old foundation-steps, open, sweeping broad from side to side for all who came; unwalled, undivided, sunned all along by the westering day, lighted only by the moon and the stars at night; falling steep and many down the hillside—ceasing one by one, at last wide and few towards the level—and worn by pilgrim

feet, for six hundred years. So I once saw them, and twice,—such things can now be never seen more.

Nor even of the west front itself, above, is much of the old masonry left: but in the porches, nearly all,—except the actual outside facing, with its rose moulding, of which only a few flowers have been spared here and there.* But the sculpture has been carefully and honourably kept and restored to its place —pedestals or niches restored here and there with clay; or some which you see white and crude, re-carved entirely; nevertheless the impression you may receive from the whole is still what the builder meant; and I will tell you the order of its theology without further notices of its decay.

28. You will find it always well, in looking at any cathedral, to make your quarters of the compass sure, in the beginning; and to remember that, as you enter it, you are looking and advancing eastward; and that if it has three entrance porches, that on your left in

* The horizontal lowest part of the moulding between the northern and central porch is old. Compare its roses with the new ones running round the arches above—and you will know what 'Restoration' means.

entering is the northern, that on your right the southern. I shall endeavour in all my future writing of architecture, to observe the simple law of always calling the door of the north transept the north door; and that on the same side of the west front, the northern door, and so of their opposites. This will save, in the end, much printing and much confusion, for a Gothic cathedral has, almost always, these five great entrances; which may be easily, if at first attentively, recognized under the titles of the Central door (or porch), the Northern door, the Southern door, the North door, and the South door.

But when we use the terms right and left, we ought always to use them as in going *out* of the cathedral or walking down the nave,—the entire north side and aisles of the building being its right side, and the south, its left, —these terms being only used well and authoritatively, when they have reference either to the image of Christ in the apse or on the rood, or else to the central statue, whether of Christ, the Virgin, or a saint, in the west front. At Amiens, this central statue, on the 'trumeau' or supporting and dividing pillar of the central porch, is of Christ Immanuel,—God *with* us. On His right hand and His left, occupying the entire walls of the central porch, are the apostles and the four greater prophets. The twelve minor prophets stand side by side on the front, three on each of its great piers.*

The northern porch is dedicated to St. Firmin, the first Christian missionary to Amiens.

The southern porch, to the Virgin.

But these are both treated as withdrawn behind the great foundation of Christ and the Prophets; and their narrow recesses partly conceal their sculpture, until you enter them. What you have first to think of, and read, is the scripture of the great central porch, and the façade itself.

29. You have then in the centre of the front, the image of Christ Himself, receiving you: " I am the Way, the truth and the life." And the order of the attendant powers may be best understood by thinking of them as placed on Christ's right and left hand: this being also the order which the builder adopts in his

* See now the plan at the end of this chapter.

Scripture history on the façade—so that it is to be read from left to right—*i.e.* from Christ's left to Christ's right, as *He* sees it. Thus, therefore, following the order of the great statues: first in the central porch, there are six apostles on Christ's right hand, and six on His left. On His left hand, next Him, Peter; then in receding order, Andrew, James, John, Matthew, Simon; on His right hand, next Him, Paul; and in receding order, James the Bishop, Philip, Bartholomew, Thomas, and Jude. These opposite ranks of the Apostles occupy what may be called the apse or curved bay of the porch, and form a nearly semi-circular group, clearly visible as we approach. But on the sides of the porch, outside the lines of apostles, and not seen clearly till we enter the porch, are the four greater prophets. On Christ's left, Isaiah and Jeremiah; on His right, Ezekiel and Daniel.

30. Then in front, along the whole façade — read in order from Christ's left to His right—come the series of the twelve minor prophets, three to each of the four piers of the temple, beginning at the south angle with Hosea, and ending with Malachi.

As you look full at the façade in front, the statues which fill the minor porches are either obscured in their narrower recesses or withdrawn behind each other so as to be unseen. And the entire mass of the front is seen, literally, as built on the foundation of the Apostles and Prophets, Jesus Christ Himself being the chief corner-stone. Literally *that* ; for the receding Porch is a deep 'angulus,' and its mid-pillar is the 'Head of the Corner.'

Built on the foundation of the Apostles and Prophets, that is to say of the Prophets who foretold *Christ*, and the Apostles who declared Him. Though Moses was an Apostle, of *God*, he is not here—though Elijah was a Prophet, of *God*, he is not here. The voice of the entire building is that of the Heaven at the Transfiguration, " This is my beloved Son, hear ye Him."

31. There is yet another and a greater prophet still, who, as it seems at first, is not here. Shall the people enter the gates of the temple, singing " Hosanna to the Son of *David*"; and see no image of His father, then ?—Christ Himself declare, " I am the

root and the offspring of David"; and yet the Root have no sign near it of its Earth?

Not so. David and his Son are together. David is the pedestal of the Christ.

32. We will begin our examination of the Temple front, therefore, with this its goodly pedestal stone. The statue of David is only two-thirds life-size, occupying the niche in front of the pedestal. He holds his sceptre in his right hand, the scroll in his left. King and Prophet, type of all Divinely right doing, and right claiming, and right proclaiming, kinghood, for ever.

The pedestal of which this statue forms the fronting or western sculpture, is square, and on the two sides of it are two flowers in vases, on its north side the lily, and on its south the rose. And the entire monolith is one of the noblest pieces of Christian sculpture in the world.

Above this pedestal comes a minor one, bearing in front of it a tendril of vine which completes the floral symbolism of the whole. The plant which I have called a lily is not the Fleur de Lys, nor the Madonna's, but an ideal one with bells like the crown Imperial

(Shakespeare's type of 'lilies of all kinds'), representing the *mode of growth* of the lily of the valley, which could not be sculptured so large in its literal form without appearing monstrous, and is exactly expressed in this tablet—as it fulfils, together with the rose and vine, its companions, the triple saying of Christ, "I am the Rose of Sharon, and the Lily of the Valley." "I am the true Vine."

33. On the side of the upper stone are supporters of a different character. Supporters, —not captives nor victims; the Cockatrice and Adder. Representing the most active evil principles of the earth, as in their utmost malignity; still, Pedestals of Christ, and even in their deadly life, accomplishing His final will.

Both creatures are represented accurately in the mediæval traditional form, the cockatrice half dragon, half cock; the deaf adder laying one ear against the ground and stopping the other with her tail.

The first represents the infidelity of Pride. The cockatrice—king serpent or highest serpent —saying that he *is* God, and *will be* God.

The second, the infidelity of Death. The adder (nieder or nether snake) saying that he *is* mud, and *will be* mud.

34. Lastly, and above all, set under the feet of the statue of Christ Himself, are the lion and dragon; the images of Carnal sin, or *Human* sin, as distinguished from the Spiritual and Intellectual sin of Pride, by which the angels also fell.

To desire kingship rather than servantship—the Cockatrice's sin; or deaf Death rather than hearkening Life—the Adder's sin,—these are both possible to all the intelligences of the universe. But the distinctively Human sins, anger and lust, seeds in our race of their perpetual sorrow—Christ in His own humanity, conquered; and conquers in His disciples. Therefore His foot is on the heads of these; and the prophecy, "Inculcabis super Leonem et Aspidem," is recognized always as fulfilled in Him, and in all His true servants, according to the height of their authority, and the truth of their power.

35. In this mystic sense, Alexander III. used the words, in restoring peace to Italy, and giving forgiveness to her deadliest enemy,

under the porch of St. Mark's.* But the meaning of every act, as of every art, of the Christian ages, lost now for three hundred years, cannot but be in our own times read reversed, if at all, through the counter-spirit which we now have reached ; glorifying Pride and Avarice as the virtues by which all things move and have their being—walking after our own lusts as our sole guides to salvation, and foaming out our own shame for the sole earthly product of our hands and lips.

36. Of the statue of Christ, itself, I will not speak here at any length, as no sculpture would satisfy, or ought to satisfy, the hope of any loving soul that has learned to trust in Him; but at the time, it was beyond what till then had been reached in sculptured tenderness; and was known far and near as the "Beau Dieu d'Amiens."† Yet understood, observe, just as clearly to be no more than a symbol of the Heavenly Presence,

---

* See my abstract of the history of Barbarossa and Alexander, in 'Fiction, Fair and Foul,' *Nineteenth Century*, November, 1880, pp. 752 *seq*. (See "On the Old Road," Vol. II., p. 3.)

† See account, and careful drawing of it, in Viollet le Duc—article "Christ," Dict. of Architecture, iii. 245.

as the poor coiling worms below were no more than symbols of the demoniac ones. No *idol*, in our sense of the word—only a letter, or sign of the Living Spirit,—which, however, was indeed conceived by every worshipper as here meeting him at the temple gate: the Word of Life, the King of Glory, and the Lord of Hosts.

"Dominus Virtutum," "Lord of Virtues," * is the best single rendering of the idea conveyed to a well-taught disciple in the thirteenth century by the words of the twenty-fourth Psalm.

37. Under the feet of His apostles, therefore, in the quatrefoil medallions of the foundation, are represented the virtues which each Apostle taught, or in his life manifested;—it may have been, sore tried, and failing in the very

---

* See the circle of the Powers of the Heavens in the Byzantine rendering. I. Wisdom; II. Thrones; III. Dominations; IV. Angels; V. Archangels; VI. Virtues; VII. Potentates; VIII. Princes; IX. Seraphim. In the Gregorian order, (Dante, 'Par.,' xxviii., Cary's note,) the Angels and Archangels are separated, giving altogether nine orders, but not ranks. Note that in the Byzantine circle the cherubim are first, and that it is the strength of the Virtues which calls on the dead to rise ('St. Mark's Rest,' p. 97, and pp. 158, 159).

St. Paul,	Faith.	
St. James the Bishop,	Hope.	
St. Philip,	Charity.	
St. Bartholomew,	Chastity.	
St. Thomas,	Wisdom.	
St. Jude,	Humility.	
	Courage,	St. Peter.
	Patience,	St. Andrew.
	Gentillesse,	St. James.
	Love,	St. John.
	Obedience,	St. Matthew.
	Perseverance,	St. Simon.

strength of the character which he afterwards perfected. Thus St. Peter, denying in fear, is afterwards the Apostle of courage; and St. John, who, with his brother, would have burnt the inhospitable village, is afterwards the Apostle of love. Understanding this, you see that in the sides of the porch, the apostles with their special virtues stand thus in opposite ranks.

Now you see how these virtues answer to each other in their opposite ranks. Remember the left-hand side is always the first, and see how the left-hand virtues lead to the right-hand —

Courage	to	Faith.
Patience	to	Hope.
Gentillesse	to	Charity.
Love	to	Chastity.
Obedience	to	Wisdom.
Perseverance	to	Humility.

38. Note farther that the Apostles are all tranquil, nearly all with books, some with crosses, but all with the same message,— "Peace be to this house. And if the Son of Peace be there," etc.*

* The modern slang name for a priest, among the mob of France, is a 'Pax Vobiscum,' or shortly, a Vobiscum.

But the Prophets—all seeking, or wistful, or tormented, or wondering, or praying, except only Daniel. The *most* tormented is Isaiah; spiritually sawn asunder. No scene of his martyrdom below, but his seeing the Lord in His temple, and yet feeling he had unclean lips. Jeremiah also carries his cross—but more serenely.

39. And now I give, in clear succession, the order of the statues of the whole front, with the subjects of the quatrefoils beneath each of them, marking the upper quatrefoil A, the lower B. The six prophets who stand at the angles of the porches, Amos, Obadiah, Micah, Nahum, Zephaniah, and Haggai, have each of them four quatrefoils, marked, A and C the upper ones, B and D the lower.

Beginning, then, on the left-hand side of the central porch, and reading outwards, you have—

    1. ST. PETER.
        A. Courage.
        B. Cowardice.
    2. ST. ANDREW.
        A. Patience.
        B. Anger.

IV. INTERPRETATIONS.

3. ST. JAMES.
    A. Gentillesse.
    B. Churlishness.

4. ST. JOHN.
    A. Love.
    B. Discord.

5. ST. MATTHEW.
    A. Obedience.
    B. Rebellion.

6. ST. SIMON.
    A. Perseverance.
    B. Atheism.

Now, right-hand side of porch, reading outwards:

7. ST. PAUL.
    A. Faith.
    B. Idolatry.

8. ST. JAMES, BISHOP.
    A. Hope.
    B. Despair.

9. ST. PHILIP.
    A. Charity.
    B. Avarice.

10. ST. BARTHOLOMEW.
    A. Chastity.
    B. Lust.

11. ST. THOMAS.
    A. Wisdom.
    B. Folly.

12. ST. JUDE.
    A. Humility.
    B. Pride.

Now, left-hand side again—the two outermost statues :

13. ISAIAH.
    A. "I saw the Lord sitting upon a throne." vi. 1.
    B. "Lo, this hath touched thy lips." vi. 7.

14. JEREMIAH.
    A. The Burial of the Girdle. xiii. 4, 5.
    B. The Breaking of the Yoke. xxviii. 10.

Right-hand side :

15. EZEKIEL.
    A. Wheel within wheel. i. 16.
    B. "Son of man, set thy face toward Jerusalem." xxi. 2.

16. DANIEL.
    A. "He hath shut the lions' mouths." vi. 22.
    B. "In the same hour came forth fingers of a man's hand." v. 5.

40. Now, beginning on the left-hand side (southern side) of the entire façade, and reading it straight across, not turning into the porches at all except for the paired quatrefoils :

17. HOSEA.

    A. "So I bought her to me for fifteen pieces of silver." iii. 2.
    B. "So will I also be for thee." iii. 3.

18. JOEL.

    A. The Sun and Moon lightless. ii. 10.
    B. The Fig-tree and Vine leafless. i. 7.

19. AMOS.

To the front
{
    A. "The Lord will cry from Zion." i. 2.
    B. "The habitations of the shepherds shall mourn." i. 2.
}

Inside porch
{
    C. The Lord with the mason's line. vii. 8.
    D. The place where it rained not. iv. 7.
}

20. OBADIAH.

Inside porch
- A. "I hid them in a cave." 1 Kings xviii. 13.
- B. "He fell on his face." xviii. 7.

To the front
- C. The captain of fifty.
- D. The messenger.

21. JONAH.
- A. Escaped from the sea.
- B. Under the gourd.

22. MICAH.

To the front
- A. The Tower of the Flock. iv. 8.
- B. Each shall rest, and "none shall make them afraid." iv. 4.

Inside porch
- C. "Swords into ploughshares." iv. 3.
- D. "Spears into pruning-hooks." iv. 3.

23. NAHUM.

Inside porch
- A. "None shall look back." ii. 8.
- B. "The burden of Nineveh." i. 1.

To the front
- C. Thy princes and thy great ones. iii. 17.
- D. Untimely figs. iii. 12.

IV. INTERPRETATIONS.

24. HABAKKUK.
    A. "I will watch to see what He will say." ii. 1.
    B. The ministry to Daniel.

25. ZEPHANIAH.

To the front
- A. The Lord strikes Ethiopia. ii. 12.
- B. The beasts in Nineveh. ii. 15.

Inside porch
- C. The Lord visits Jerusalem. i. 12.
- D. The Hedgehog and Bittern.* ii. 14.

26. HAGGAI.

Inside porch
- A. The houses of the princes, *ornées de lambris.* i. 4.
- B. "The heaven is stayed from dew." i. 10.

To the front
- C. The Lord's temple desolate. i. 4.
- D. "Thus saith the Lord of Hosts." i. 7.

27. ZECHARIAH.
    A. The lifting up of Iniquity. v. 6-9.
    B. "The angel that spake to me." iv. 1.

* See the Septuagint version.

28. MALACHI.
- A. "Ye have wounded the Lord."   ii. 17.
- B. "This commandment is to *you*."   ii. 1.

41. Having thus put the sequence of the statues and their quatrefoils briefly before the spectator—(in case the railway time presses, it may be a kindness to him to note that if he walks from the east end of the cathedral down the street to the south, Rue St. Denis, it takes him by the shortest line to the station)—I will begin again with St. Peter, and interpret the sculptures in the quatrefoils a little more fully. Keeping the fixed numerals for indication of the statues, St. Peter's quatrefoils will be 1 A and 1 B, and Malachi's 28 A and 28 B.

1, A. COURAGE, with a leopard on his shield; the French and English agreeing in the reading of that symbol, down to the time of the Black Prince's leopard coinage in Aquitaine.*

---

* For a list of the photographs of the quatrefoils described in this chapter, see the appendices at the end of this volume.

1. B. COWARDICE, a man frightened at an animal darting out of a thicket, while a bird sings on. The coward has not the heart of a thrush.
2, A. PATIENCE, holding a shield with a bull on it (never giving back).*
2, B. ANGER, a woman stabbing a man with a sword. Anger is essentially a feminine vice—a man, worth calling so, may be driven to fury or insanity by *indignation*, (compare the Black Prince at Limoges,) but not by anger. Fiendish enough, often so— "Incensed with indignation, Satan stood, *unterrified*—" but in that last word is the difference; there is as much fear in Anger, as there is in Hatred.

---

* In the cathedral of Laon there is a pretty compliment paid to the oxen who carried the stones of its tower to the hill-top it stands on. The tradition is that they harnessed themselves,—but tradition does not say how an ox *can* harness himself even if he had a mind. Probably the first form of the story was only that they went joyfully, "lowing as they went." But at all events their statues are carved on the height of the tower, eight, colossal, looking from its galleries across the plains of France. See drawing in Viollet le Duc, under article "Clocher."

3, A. GENTILLESSE, bearing shield with a lamb.

3, B. CHURLISHNESS, again a woman, kicking over her cupbearer. The final forms of ultimate French churlishness being in the feminine gestures of the Cancan. See the favourite prints in shops of Paris.

4, A. LOVE; the Divine, not human love: "I in them, and Thou in me." Her shield bears a tree with many branches grafted into its cut-off stem: "In those days shall Messiah be cut off, but not for Himself."

4, B. DISCORD, a wife and husband quarrelling. She has dropped her distaff (Amiens wool manufacture, see farther on—9, A).

5, A. OBEDIENCE, bears shield with camel. Actually the most disobedient and ill-tempered of all serviceable beasts, —yet passing his life in the most painful service. I do not know how far his character was understood by the northern sculptor; but I believe he is taken as a type of burden-bearing, without joy or sympathy, such as the horse has, and without power of offence, such as the ox has. His bite is bad enough, (see Mr. Palgrave's account of him,) but presumably little known of at Amiens, even by Crusaders, who would always ride their own warhorses, or nothing.

5, B. REBELLION, a man snapping his fingers at his Bishop. (As Henry the Eighth at the Pope,—and the modern French and English cockney at all priests whatever.)

6, A. PERSEVERANCE, the grandes spiritual form of the virtue commonly called 'Fortitude.' Usually, overcoming or tearing a lion; here *caressing* one, and *holding* her crown. "Hold fast that which thou hast, that no man take thy crown."

6, B. ATHEISM, leaving his shoes at the church door. The infidel fool is always represented in twelfth and thirteenth century MS. as barefoot— the Christian having "his feet shod with the preparation of the Gospel of Peace." Compare "How beautiful are thy feet with shoes, oh Prince's Daughter!"

7, A. FAITH, holding cup with cross above it, her accepted symbol throughout ancient Europe. It is also an enduring one, for, all differences of Church put aside, the words, "Except ye eat the flesh of the Son of Man and Drink His blood, ye have no life in you," remain in their mystery, to be understood only by those who have learned the sacredness of food, in all times and places, and the laws of life and spirit, dependent on its acceptance, refusal, and distribution.

7, B. IDOLATRY, kneeling to a monster. The *contrary* of Faith — not *want* of Faith. Idolatry is faith in the wrong thing, and quite distinct from Faith in *No* thing (6, B), the "Dixit Insipiens." Very wise men may be idolaters, but they cannot be atheists.

8, A. HOPE, with Gonfalon Standard and

distant crown; as opposed to the constant crown of Fortitude (6, A).

The Gonfalon (Gund, war; fahr, standard, according to Poitevin's dictionary) is the pointed ensign of forward battle; essentially sacred; hence the constant name " Gonfaloniere " of the battle standard-bearers of the Italian republics.

Hope has it, because she fights forward always to her aim, or at least has the joy of seeing it draw nearer. Faith and Fortitude wait, as St. John in prison, but unoffended. Hope is, however, put under St. James, because of the 7th and 8th verses of his last chapter, ending " Stablish your hearts, for the coming of the Lord draweth nigh." It is he who examines Dante on the nature of Hope. 'Par.,' c. xxv., and compare Cary's notes.

8, B. DESPAIR, stabbing himself. Suicide not thought heroic or sentimental in the 13th century; and no Gothic Morgue built beside Somme.

9, A. CHARITY, bearing shield with woolly ram, and giving a mantle to a naked beggar. The old wool manufacture of Amiens having this notion of its purpose—namely, to clothe the poor first, the rich afterwards. No nonsense talked in those days about the evil consequences of indiscriminate charity.

9, B. AVARICE, with coffer and money. The modern, alike English and Amienois, notion of the Divine consummation of the wool manufacture.

10, A. CHASTITY, shield with the Phœnix.*

10, B. LUST, a too violent kiss.

11, A. WISDOM: shield with, I think, an eatable root; meaning temperance, as the beginning of wisdom.

---

* For the sake of comparing the pollution, and reversal of its once glorious religion, in the modern French mind, it is worth the reader's while to ask at M. Goyer's (Place St. Denis) for the *Journal de St. Nicholas* for 1880, and look at the 'Phénix,' as drawn on p. 610. The story is meant to be moral, and the Phœnix there represents Avarice, but the entire destruction of all sacred and poetical tradition in a child's mind by such a picture is an immorality which would neutralize a year's preaching. To make it worth M. Goyer's while to show you the number, buy the one with 'les conclusions de Jeanie' in it, p. 337: the church scene (with dialogue) in the text is lovely.

11, B. FOLLY, the ordinary type used in all early Psalters, of a glutton, armed with a club. Both this vice and virtue are the earthly wisdom and folly, completing the spiritual wisdom and folly opposite under St. Matthew. Temperance, the complement of Obedience, and Covetousness, with violence, that of Atheism.

12, A. HUMILITY, shield with dove.

12, B. PRIDE, falling from his horse.

42. All these quatrefoils are rather symbolic than representative; and, since their purpose was answered enough if their sign was understood, they have been entrusted to a much inferior workman than the one who carved the now sequent series under the Prophets. Most of these subjects represent an historical fact, or a scene spoken of by the prophet as a real vision; and they have in general been executed by the ablest hands at the architect's command.

With the interpretation of these, I have given again the name of the prophet whose life or prophecy they illustrate.

13. ISAIAH.

13, A. "I saw the Lord sitting upon a throne" (vi. 1).

The vision of the throne "high and lifted up" between seraphim.

13, B. "Lo, this hath touched thy lips" (vi. 7).

The Angel stands before the prophet, and holds, or rather held, the coal with tongs, which have been finely undercut, but are now broken away, only a fragment remaining in his hand.

14. JEREMIAH.

14, A. The burial of the girdle (xiii. 4, 5).

The prophet is digging by the shore of Euphrates, represented by vertically winding furrows down the middle of the tablet. Note, the translation should be "hole in the ground," not "rock."

14, B. The breaking of the yoke (xxviii. 10).

From the prophet Jeremiah's neck; it is here represented as a doubled and redoubled chain.

15. Ezekiel.

15, A. Wheel within wheel (i. 16).

> The prophet sitting; before him two wheels of equal size, one involved in the ring of the other.

15, B. "Son of man, set thy face toward Jerusalem" (xxi. 2).

> The prophet before the gate of Jerusalem.

16. Daniel.

16, A. "He hath shut the lions' mouths" (vi. 22).

> Daniel holding a book, the lions treated as heraldic supporters. The subject is given with more animation farther on in the series (24, B).

16, B. "In the same hour came forth fingers of a man's hand" (v. 5).

> Belshazzar's feast represented by the king alone, seated at a small oblong table. Beside him the youth Daniel, looking only fifteen or sixteen, graceful and gentle, interprets. At the side of the quatrefoil, out of a small wreath of cloud, comes a

small bent hand, writing, as if with a pen upside down on a piece of Gothic wall.*

For modern bombast as opposed to old simplicity, compare the Belshazzar's feast of John Martin!

43. The next subject begins the series of the minor prophets.

17. HOSEA.

17, A. "So I bought her to me for fifteen pieces of silver and an homer of barley" (iii. 2).

The prophet pouring the grain and the silver into the lap of the woman, "beloved of her friend." The carved coins are each wrought with the cross, and, I believe, legend of the French contemporary coin.

17, B. "So will I also be for thee" (iii. 3).

He puts a ring on her finger.

18. JOEL.

18, A. The son and moon lightless (ii. 10).

---

* I fear this hand has been broken since I described it; at all events, it is indistinguishably shapeless in the photograph (No. 9 of the series).

The sun and moon as two small flat pellets, up in the external moulding.

18, B. The barked fig-tree and waste vine (i. 7).

Note the continual insistence on the blight of vegetation as a Divine punishment (19, D).

19. Amos.

To the front.

19, A. "The Lord will cry from Zion" (i. 2).

Christ appears with crossletted nimbus.

19, B. "The habitations of the shepherds shall mourn" (i. 2).

Amos with the shepherd's hooked or knotted staff, and wicker-worked bottle, before his tent. (Architecture in right-hand foil restored.)

Inside Porch.

19, C. The Lord with the mason's line (vii. 8).

Christ, again here, and henceforward always, with crosslet nimbus, has a large trowel in His hand, which He lays on the top of a half-built wall. There seems a line twisted round the handle.

19, D. The place where it rained not (iv. 7).

Amos is gathering the leaves of the fruitless vine, to feed the sheep, who find no grass. One of the finest of the reliefs.

20. OBADIAH.

Inside Porch.

20, A. "I hid them in a cave" (1 Kings xviii. 13).

Three prophets at the mouth of a well, to whom Obadiah brings loaves.

20, B. "He fell on his face" (xviii. 7).

He kneels before Elijah, who wears his rough mantle.

To the front.

20, C. The captain of fifty.

Elijah (?) speaking to an armed man under a tree.

20, D. The messenger.

A messenger on his knees before a king. I cannot interpret these two scenes (20 C and 20 D). The uppermost *may* mean the dialogue of

Elijah with the captains, (2 Kings i. 9,) and the lower one, the return of the messengers (2 Kings i. 5).

21. JONAH.

21, A. Escaped from the sea.

21, B. Under the gourd. A small grasshopper-like beast gnawing the gourd stem. I should like to know what insects *do* attack the Amiens gourds. This may be an entomological study, for aught we know.

22. MICAH.

To the front.

22, A. The Tower of the Flock (iv. 8).

The tower is wrapped in clouds, God appearing above it.

22, B. Each shall rest, and "none shall make them afraid" (iv. 4).

A man and his wife "under his vine and fig-tree."

Inside Porch.

22, C. "Swords into ploughshares" (iv. 3).

Nevertheless, two hundred years after these medallions were cut, the sword manufacture had become a staple in Amiens! Not to her advantage.

22, D. "Spears into pruning-hooks" (iv. 3).

23. NAHUM.

Inside Porch

23, A. "None shall look back" (ii. 8).
23, B. "The burden of Nineveh" (i. 1).*

To the front.

23, C. Thy princes and thy great ones (iii. 17).

23 A, B, and C are all incapable of sure interpretation. The prophet in A is pointing down to a little hill, said by the Père Rozé to be covered with grasshoppers. I can only copy what he says of them.

---

* The statue of the prophet, above, is the grandest of the entire series; and note especially the "diadema" of his own luxuriant hair plaited like a maiden's, indicating the Achillean force of this most terrible of the prophets. (Compare 'Fors Clavigera,' Letter LXV., page 157.) For the rest, this long flowing hair was always one of the insignia of the Frankish kings, and their way of dressing both hair and beard may be seen more nearly and definitely in the angle-sculptures of the long font in the north transept, the most interesting piece of work in the whole cathedral, in an antiquarian sense, and of much artistic value also. (See ante, chap. ii., p. 86.)

23, D. Untimely figs (iii. 12).

Three people beneath a fig-tree catch its falling fruit in their mouths.

24. HABAKKUK.

24, A. "I will watch to see what He will say unto me" (ii. 1).

The prophet is writing on his tablet to Christ's dictation.

24, B. The ministry to Daniel.

The traditional visit to Daniel. An angel carries Habakkuk by the hair of his head; the prophet has a loaf of bread in each hand. They break through the roof of the cave. Daniel is stroking one young lion on the back; the head of another is thrust carelessly under his arm. Another is gnawing bones in the bottom of the cave.

25. ZEPHANIAH.

To the front.

25, A. The Lord strikes Ethiopia (ii. 12).

Christ striking a city with a sword. Note that all violent actions are in these bas-reliefs feebly or ludicrously expressed; quiet ones always right.

25, B. The beasts in Nineveh (ii. 15).

Very fine. All kinds of crawling things among the tottering walls, and peeping out of their rents and crannies. A monkey sitting squat, developing into a demon, reverses the Darwinian theory.

Inside Porch.

25, C. The Lord visits Jerusalem (i. 12).

Christ passing through the streets of Jerusalem, with a lantern in each hand.

25, D. The Hedgehog and Bittern * (ii. 14).

With a singing bird in a cage in the window.

26. HAGGAI.

Inside Porch.

26, A. The houses of the princes, *ornées de lambris* (i. 4).

A perfectly built house of square

---

* See ante, p. 215. note.

stones gloomily strong, the grating (of a prison?) in front of foundation.

26, B. "The heaven is stayed from dew" (i. 10).

The heavens as a projecting mass, with stars, sun, and moon on surface. Underneath, two withered trees.

To the front.

26, C. The Lord's temple desolate (i. 4).

The falling of the temple, "not one stone left on another," grandly loose. Square stones again. Examine the text (i. 6).

26, D. "Thus saith the Lord of Hosts" (i. 7).

Christ pointing up to His ruined temple.

27. ZECHARIAH.

27, A. The lifting up of Iniquity (v. 6 to 9).

Wickedness in the Ephah.

27, B. "The angel that spake to me" (iv. 1).

The prophet almost reclining, a glorious winged angel hovering out of cloud.

28. MALACHI.

28, A. "Ye have wounded the Lord" (ii. 17).

>The priests are thrusting Christ through with a barbed lance, whose point comes out at His back.

28, B. "This commandment is to *you*" (ii. 1.)

>In these panels, the undermost is often introductory to the one above, an illustration of it. It is perhaps chapter i., verse 6, that is meant to be spoken here by the sitting figure of Christ, to the indignant priests.

44. With this bas-relief terminates the series of sculpture in illustration of Apostolic and Prophetic teaching, which constitutes what I mean by the "Bible" of Amiens. But the two lateral porches contain supplementary subjects necessary for completion of the pastoral and traditional teaching addressed to her people in that day.

The Northern Porch, dedicated to her first missionary St. Firmin, has on its central pier his statue ; above, on the flat field of the back of the arch, the story of the finding of his body; on the sides of the porch, companion saints and angels in the following order:—

CENTRAL STATUE.
St. Firmin.

Southern (left) side.

41. St. Firmin the Confessor.
42. St. Domice.
43. St. Honoré.
44. St. Salve.
45. St. Quentin.
46. St. Gentian.

Northern (right) side.

47. St. Geoffroy.
48. An angel.
49. St. Fuscien, martyr.
50. St. Victoric, martyr.
51. An angel.
52. St. Ulpha.

45. Of these saints, excepting St. Firmin and St. Honoré, of whom I have already spoken,* St. Geoffroy is more real for us than

---

* See ante, Chap. I., pp. 8, 9, for the history of St. Firmin, and for St. Honoré, p. 177, § 8 of this chapter, with the reference there given.

the rest; he was born in the year of the battle of Hastings, at Molincourt in the Soissonais, and was Bishop of Amiens from 1104 to 1150. A man of entirely simple, pure, and right life: one of the severest of ascetics, but without gloom—always gentle and merciful. Many miracles are recorded of him, but all indicating a tenour of life which was chiefly miraculous by its justice and peace. Consecrated at Rheims, and attended by a train of other bishops and nobles to his diocese, he dismounts from his horse at St. Acheul, the place of St. Firmin's first tomb, and walks barefoot to his cathedral, along the causeway now so defaced: at another time he walks barefoot from Amiens to Picquigny to ask from the Vidame of Amiens the freedom of the Chatelain Adam. He maintained the privileges of the citizens, with the help of Louis le Gros, against the Count of Amiens, defeated him, and razed his castle; nevertheless, the people not enough obeying him in the order of their life, he blames his own weakness, rather than theirs, and retires to the Grande Chartreuse, holding himself unfit to be their bishop. The Carthusian superior questioning him on his reasons for retirement, and asking if he had ever sold the offices of the Church, the Bishop answered, "My father, my hands are pure of simony, but I have a thousand times allowed myself to be seduced by praise."

46. St. Firmin the Confessor was the son of the Roman senator who received St. Firmin himself. He preserved the tomb of the martyr in his father's garden, and at last built a church over it, dedicated to Our Lady of Martyrs, which was the first episcopal seat of Amiens, at St. Acheul, spoken of above. St. Ulpha was an Amienoise girl, who lived in a chalk cave above the marshes of the Somme;—if ever Mr. Murray provides you with a comic guide to Amiens, no doubt the enlightened composer of it will count much on your enjoyment of the story of her being greatly disturbed at her devotions by the frogs, and praying them silent. You are now, of course, wholly superior to such follies, and are sure that God cannot, or will not, so much as shut a frog's mouth for you. Remember, therefore, that as He also now leaves open the mouth of the liar, blasphemer, and betrayer, you must shut

your own ears against *their* voices as you can.

Of her name, St. Wolf—or Guelph—see again Miss Yonge's Christian names. Our tower of Wolf's stone, Ulverstone, and Kirk of Ulpha, are, I believe, unconscious of Picard relatives.

47. The other saints in this porch are all in like manner provincial, and, as it were, personal friends of the Amienois; and under them, the quatrefoils represent the pleasant order of the guarded and hallowed year—the zodiacal signs above, and labours of the months below; little differing from the constant representations of them—except in the May: see next page. The Libra also is a little unusual in the female figure holding the scales; the lion epecially good-tempered—and the 'reaping' one of the most beautiful figures in the whole series of sculptures; several of the others peculiarly refined and far-wrought. In Mr. Kaltenbacher's photographs, as I have arranged them, the bas-reliefs may be studied nearly as well as in the porch itself. Their order is as follows, beginning with December, in the left-hand inner corner of the porch :—

IV. INTERPRETATIONS.

41. DECEMBER.—Killing and scalding swine. Above, Capricorn with quickly diminishing tail; I cannot make out the accessories.

42. JANUARY.—Twin-headed, obsequiously served. Aquarius feebler than most of the series.

43. FEBRUARY.—Very fine; warming his feet and putting coals on fire. Fish above, elaborate but uninteresting.

44. MARCH.—At work in vine-furrows. Aries careful, but rather stupid.

45. APRIL.—Feeding his hawk—very pretty. Taurus above with charming leaves to eat.

46. MAY.—Very singularly, a middle-aged man sitting under the trees to hear the birds sing; and Gemini above, a bridegroom and bride. This quatrefoil joins the interior angle ones of Zephaniah.

52. JUNE.—Opposite, joining the interior angle ones of Haggai. Mowing. Note the lovely flowers sculptured all through the grass. Cancer above, with his shell superbly modelled.

51. JULY.—Reaping. Extremely beautiful. The smiling lion completes the evidence that all the seasons and signs are regarded as alike blessing and providentially kind.

50. AUGUST. — Threshing. Virgo above, holding a flower, her drapery very modern and confused for thirteenth-century work.

49. SEPTEMBER.—I am not sure of his action, whether pruning, or in some way gathering fruit from the full-leaved tree. Libra above; charming.

48. OCTOBER.—Treading grapes. Scorpio, a very traditional and gentle form—forked in the tail indeed, but stingless.

47. NOVEMBER.—Sowing, with Sagittarius, half concealed when this photograph was taken by the beautiful arrangements always now going on for some job or other in French cathedrals:—they never can let them alone for ten minutes.

48. And now, last of all, if you care to see it, we will go into the Madonna's porch —only, if you come at all, good Protestant

feminine reader—come civilly: and be pleased to recollect, if you have, in known history, material for recollection, this (or if you cannot recollect—be you very solemnly assured of this): that neither Madonna-worship, nor Lady-worship of any sort, whether of dead ladies or living ones, ever did any human creature any harm,—but that Money worship, Wig worship, Cocked-Hat-and-Feather worship, Plate worship, Pot worship and Pipe worship, have done, and are doing, a great deal,—and that any of these, and all, are quite million-fold more offensive to the God of Heaven and Earth and the Stars, than all the absurdest and lovingest mistakes made by any generations of His simple children, about what the Virgin-mother could, or would, or might do, or feel for them.

49. And next, please observe this broad historical fact about the three sorts of Madonnas.

There is first the Madonna Dolorosa; the Byzantine type, and Cimabue's. It is the noblest of all; and the earliest, in distinct popular influence.*

---

* See the description of the Madonna of Murano, in second volume of 'Stones of Venice.'

Secondly. The Madone Reine, who is essentially the Frank and Norman one; crowned, calm, and full of power and gentleness. She is the one represented in this porch.

Thirdly. The Madone Nourrice, who is the Raphaelesque and generally late and decadence one. She is seen here in a good French type in the south transept porch, as before noticed.

An admirable comparison will be found instituted by M. Viollet le Duc (the article 'Vierge,' in his dictionary, is altogether deserving of the most attentive study) between this statue of the Queen-Madonna of the southern porch and the Nurse-Madonna of the transept. I may perhaps be able to get a photograph made of his two drawings, side by side: but, if I can, the reader will please observe that he has a little flattered the Queen, and a little vulgarized the Nurse, which is not fair. The statue in this porch is in thirteenth-century style, extremely good: but there is no reason for making any fuss about it—the earlier Byzantine types being far grander.

50. The Madonna's story, in its main incidents, is told in the series of statues round

the porch, and in the quatrefoils below—several of which refer, however, to a legend about the Magi to which I have not had access, and I am not sure of their interpretation.

The large statues are on the left hand, reading outwards as usual.

>**29.** The Angel Gabriel.
>**30.** Virgin Annunciate.
>**31.** Virgin Visitant.
>**32.** St. Elizabeth.
>**33.** Virgin in Presentation.
>**34.** St. Simeon.

On the right hand, reading outward,

>**35, 36, 37.** The three Kings.
>**38.** Herod.
>**39.** Solomon.
>**40.** The Queen of Sheba.

51. I am not sure of rightly interpreting the introduction of these two last statues: but I believe the idea of the designer was that virtually the Queen Mary visited Herod when she sent, or had sent for her, the Magi to tell him of her presence at Bethlehem: and the contrast between Solomon's reception of the

Queen of Sheba, and Herod's driving out the Madonna into Egypt, is dwelt on throughout this side of the porch, with their several consequences to the two Kings and to the world.

The quatrefoils underneath the great statues run as follows:

29. Under Gabriel—
- A. Daniel seeing the stone cut out without hands.
- B. Moses and the burning bush.

30. Under Virgin Annunciate—
- A. Gideon and the dew on the fleece.
- B. Moses with written law, retiring; Aaron, dominant, points to his budding rod.

31. Under Virgin Visitant—
- A. The message to Zacharias: "Fear not, for thy prayer is heard."
- B. The dream of Joseph: "Fear not to take unto thee Mary thy wife." (?)

32. Under St. Elizabeth—
- A. The silence of Zacharias: "They perceived that he had seen a vision in the temple."

B. "There is none of thy kindred that is called by this name." "He wrote saying, His name is John."

33. Under Virgin in Presentation—
    A. Flight into Egypt.
    B. Christ with the Doctors.

34. Under St. Simeon—
    A. Fall of the idols in Egypt.
    B. The return to Nazareth.

These two last quatrefoils join the beautiful C and D of Amos.

Then on the opposite side, under the Queen of Sheba, and joining the A and B of Obadiah—

40.
    A. Solomon entertains the Queen of Sheba. The Grace cup.
    B. Solomon teaches the Queen of Sheba, "God is above."

39. Under Solomon—
    A. Solomon on his throne of judgment.
    B. Solomon praying before his temple-gate.

38. Under Herod—
  A. Massacre of Innocents.
  B. Herod orders the ship of the Kings to be burned.

37. Under the third King—
  A. Herod inquires of the Kings.
  B. Burning of the ship.

36. Under the second King—
  A. Adoration in Bethlehem ?— not certain.
  B. The voyage of the Kings.

35. Under the first King—
  A. The Star in the East.
  B. "Being warned in a dream that they should not return to Herod."

I have no doubt of finding out in time the real sequence of these subjects: but it is of little import,—this group of quatrefoils being of less interest than the rest, and that of the Massacre of the Innocents curiously illustrative of the incapability of the sculptor to give strong action or passion.

But into questions respecting the art of

these bas-reliefs I do not here attempt to enter. They were never intended to serve as more than signs, or guides to thought. And if the reader follows this guidance quietly, he may create for himself better pictures in his heart; and at all events may recognize these following general truths, as their united message.

52. First, that throughout the Sermon on this Amiens Mount, Christ never appears, or is for a moment thought of, as the Crucified, nor as the Dead: but as the Incarnate Word—as the present Friend—as the Prince of Peace on Earth,—and as the Everlasting King in Heaven. What His life *is*, what His commands *are*, and what His judgment *will be*, are the things here taught: not what He once did, nor what He once suffered, but what He is now doing—and what He requires us to do. That is the pure, joyful, beautiful lesson of Christianity; and the fall from that faith, and all the corruptions of its abortive practice, may be summed briefly as the habitual contemplation of Christ's death instead of His Life, and the substitution of His past suffering for our present duty.

53. Then, secondly, though Christ bears

not *His* cross, the mourning prophets,—the persecuted apostles—and the martyred disciples *do* bear theirs. For just as it is well for you to remember what your undying Creator is *doing* for you—it is well for you to remember what your dying fellow-creatures *have done:* the Creator you may at your pleasure deny or defy—the Martyr you can only forget; deny, you cannot. Every stone of this building is cemented with his blood, and there is no furrow of its pillars that was not ploughed by his pain.

54. Keeping, then, these things in your heart, look back now to the central statue of Christ, and hear His message with understanding. He holds the Book of the Eternal Law in His left hand; with His right He blesses,—but blesses on condition. "This do, and thou shalt live;" nay, in stricter and more piercing sense, This *be*, and thou shalt live: to show Mercy is nothing—thy soul must be full of mercy; to be pure in act is nothing—thou shalt be pure in heart also.

And with this further word of the unabolished law—"This if thou do *not*, this if thou art not, thou shalt die."

55. Die (whatever Death means) — totally and irrevocably. There is no word in thirteenth-century Theology of the pardon (in our modern sense) of sins; and there is none of the Purgatory of them. Above that image of Christ with us, our Friend, is set the image of Christ over us, our Judge. For this present life—here is His helpful Presence. After this life—there is His coming to take account of our deeds, and of our desires in them; and the parting asunder of the Obedient from the Disobedient, of the Loving from the Unkind, with no hope given to the last of recall or reconciliation. I do not know what commenting or softening doctrines were written in frightened minuscule by the Fathers, or hinted in hesitating whispers by the prelates of the early Church. But I know that the language of every graven stone and every glowing window,—of things daily seen and universally understood by the people, was absolutely and alone, this teaching of Moses from Sinai in the beginning, and of St. John from Patmos in the end, of the Revelation of God to Israel.

This it was, simply—sternly—and continually, for the great three hundred years of Christianity in her strength (eleventh, twelfth, and thirteenth centuries), and over the whole breadth and depth of her dominion, from Iona to Cyrene,—and from Calpe to Jerusalem. At what time the doctrine of Purgatory was openly accepted by Catholic Doctors, I neither know nor care to know. It was first formalized by Dante, but never accepted for an instant by the sacred artist teachers of his time—or by those of any great school or time whatsoever.*

* The most authentic foundations of the Purgatorial scheme in art-teaching are in the renderings, subsequent to the thirteenth century, of the verse " by which also He went and preached unto the spirits in prison," forming gradually into the idea of the deliverance of the waiting saints from the power of the grave.

In literature and tradition, the idea is originally, I believe, Platonic; certainly not Homeric. Egyptian possibly—but I have read nothing yet of the recent discoveries in Egypt. Not, however, quite liking to leave the matter in the complete emptiness of my own resources, I have appealed to my general investigator, Mr. Anderson (James R.), who writes as follows:—

"There is no possible question about the doctrine and universal inculcation of it, ages before Dante. Curiously enough, though, the statement of it in the Summa Theologiæ as we have it is a later insertion; but I find by references that St. Thomas teaches it elsewhere.

56. Neither do I know nor care to know—at what time the notion of Justification by Faith, in the modern sense, first got itself distinctively fixed in the minds of the heretical

Albertus Magnus developes it at length. If you refer to the 'Golden Legend' under All Souls' Day, you will see how the idea is assumed as a commonplace in a work meant for popular use in the thirteenth century. St. Gregory (the Pope) argues for it (Dial. iv. 38) on two scriptural quotations : (1), the sin that is forgiven neither in hôc sæculo *nor in that which is to come* ,and (2), the fire which shall try every man's work. I think Platonic philosophy and the Greek mysteries must have had a good deal to do with introducing the idea originally; but with them —as to Virgil—it was part of the Eastern vision of a circling stream of life from which only a few drops were at intervals tossed to a definitely permanent Elysium or a definitely permanent Hell. It suits that scheme better than it does the Christian one, which attaches ultimately in all cases infinite importance to the results of life in hôc sæculo.

"Do you know any representation of Heaven or Hell unconnected with the Last Judgment? I don't remember any, and as Purgatory is by that time past, this would account for the absence of pictures of it.

"Besides, Purgatory precedes the Resurrection—there is continual question among divines what manner of purgatorial fire it may be that affects spirits separate from the body — perhaps Heaven and Hell, as opposed to Purgatory, were felt to be picturable because not only spirits, but the risen bodies too are conceived in them.

"Bede's account of the Ayrshire seer's vision gives Purgatory in words very like Dante's description of the second stormy circle in Hell; and the angel which ultimately saves the Scotchman from the fiends comes through

sects and schools of the North. Practically its strength was founded by its first authors on an asceticism which differed from monastic rule in being only able to destroy, never to build; and in endeavouring to force what severity it thought proper for itself on everybody else also; and so striving to make one artless, letterless, and merciless monastery of all the world. Its virulent effort broke down amidst furies of reactionary dissoluteness and disbelief, and remains now the basest of popular solders and plasters for every condition of broken law and bruised conscience which interest can provoke, or hypocrisy disguise.

57. With the subsequent quarrels between the two great sects of the corrupted church, about prayers for the Dead, Indulgences to the Living, Papal supremacies, or Popular liberties, no man, woman, or child need trouble themselves in studying the history of

hell, 'quasi fulgor stellæ micantis inter tenebras'—' qual sul presso del mattino Per gli grossi vapor Marte rosseggia.' Bede's name was great in the middle ages. Dante meets him in Heaven, and I like to hope, may have been helped by the vision of my fellow-countryman more than six hundred years before."

Christianity: they are nothing but the squabbles of men, and laughter of fiends among its ruins. The Life, and Gospel, and Power of it, are all written in the mighty works of its true believers: in Normandy and Sicily, on river islets of France and in the river glens of England, on the rocks of Orvieto, and by the sands of Arno. But of all, the simplest, completest, and most authoritative in its lessons to the active mind of North Europe, is this on the foundation stones of Amiens.

58. Believe it or not, reader, as you will: understand only how thoroughly it *was* once believed; and that all beautiful things were made, and all brave deeds done, in the strength of it—until what we may call 'this present time,' in which it is gravely asked whether Religion has any effect on morals, by persons who have essentially no idea whatever of the meaning of either Religion or Morality.

Concerning which dispute, this much perhaps you may have the patience finally to read, as the Flèche of Amiens fades in the distance, and your carriage rushes towards the Isle of France, which now exhibits the most admired patterns of European Art, intelligence, and behaviour.

59. All human creatures, in all ages and places of the world, who have had warm affections, common sense and self-command, have been, and are, Naturally Moral. Human nature in its fulness is necessarily Moral,—without Love, it is inhuman,—without sense,* inhuman,—without discipline, inhuman.

In the exact proportion in which men are bred capable of these things, and are educated to love, to think, and to endure, they become noble,—live happily—die calmly: are remembered with perpetual honour by their race, and for the perpetual good of it. All wise men know and have known these things, since the form of man was separated from the dust. The knowledge and enforcement of them have nothing to do with religion: a good and wise man differs from a bad and idiotic one, simply as a good dog from a cur, and as any manner of dog from a wolf or a weasel. And if you are to believe in, or preach without half believing in, a spiritual

---

* I don't mean æsthesis,—but νοῦς, if you *must* talk in Greek slang.

world or law—only in the hope that whatever you do, or anybody else does, that is foolish or beastly, may be in them and by them mended and patched and pardoned and worked up again as good as new—the less you believe in—and most solemnly, the less you talk about—a spiritual world, the better.

60. But if, loving well the creatures that are like yourself, you feel that you would love still more dearly, creatures better than yourself — were they revealed to you ; — if striving with all your might to mend what is evil, near you and around, you would fain look for a day when some Judge of all the Earth shall wholly do right, and the little hills rejoice on every side ; if, parting with the companions that have given you all the best joy you had on Earth, you desire ever to meet their eyes again and clasp their hands,— where eyes shall no more be dim, nor hands fail ;—if, preparing yourselves to lie down beneath the grass in silence and loneliness, seeing no more beauty, and feeling no more gladness—you would care for the promise to you of a time when you should see God's light again, and know the things you have

longed to know, and walk in the peace of everlasting Love—*then*, the Hope of these things to you is religion, the Substance of them in your life is Faith. And in the power of them, it is promised us, that the kingdoms of this world shall yet become the kingdoms of our Lord and of His Christ.

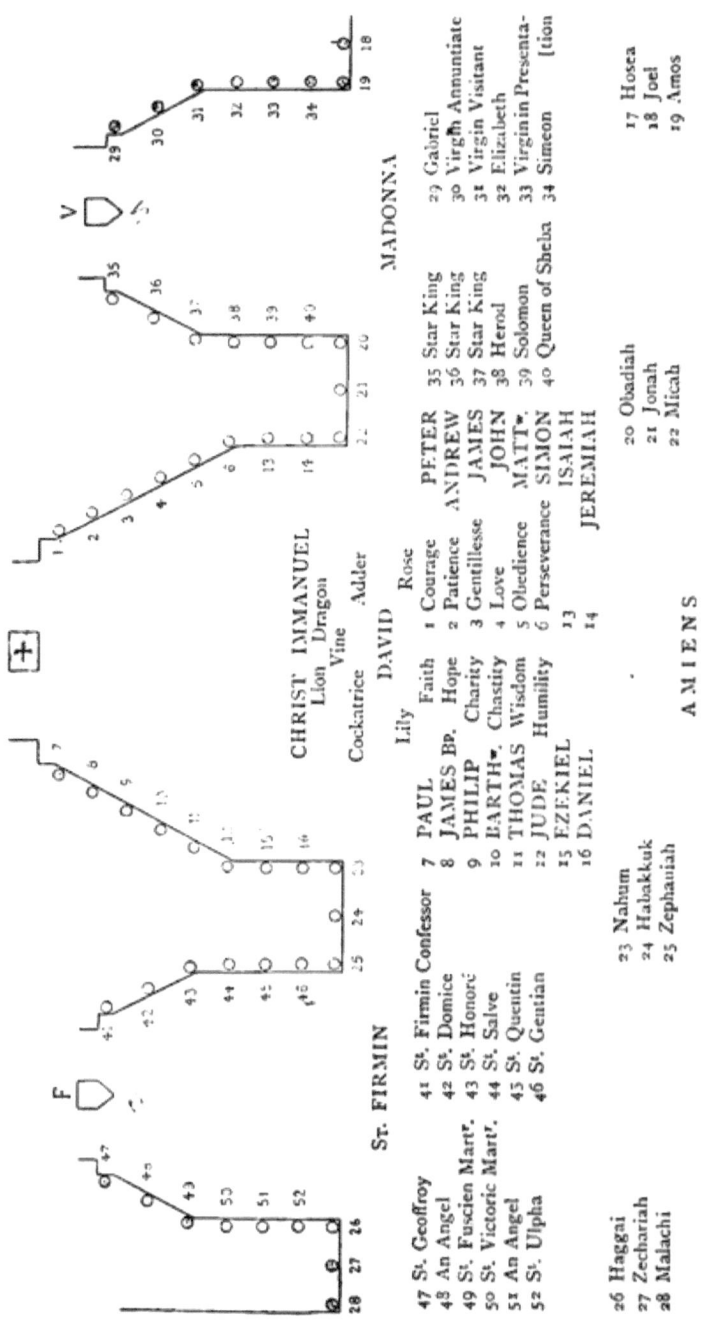

AMIENS

Plan of West Porches

APPENDICES.

I. CHRONOLOGICAL LIST OF THE PRINCIPAL EVENTS REFERRED TO IN THE 'BIBLE OF AMIENS.'

II. REFERENCES EXPLANATORY OF THE PHOTOGRAPHS ILLUSTRATING CHAPTER IV.

III. GENERAL PLAN OF 'OUR FATHERS HAVE TOLD US.'

APPENDIX I.

CHRONOLOGICAL LIST OF THE PRINCIPAL EVENTS REFERRED TO IN THE 'BIBLE OF AMIENS.'

A.D.		CHAP.	SECT.
250.	Rise of the Franks	ii.	17
301.	St. Firmin comes to Amiens	i.	6
332.	St. Martin	i.	22
345.	St. Jerome born	iii.	123
350.	First church at Amiens, over St. Firmin's grave	iv.	157
358.	Franks defeated by Julian near Strasburg	ii.	35
405.	St. Jerome's Bible	ii.	81
420.	St. Jerome dies	iii.	40
421.	St. Genevieve born. Venice founded	ii	3
445.	Franks cross the Rhine, and take Amiens	i.	10
447.	Merovée king at Amiens	i.	12
451.	Battle of Chalons. Attila defeated by Aëtius	i.	10
457.	Merovée dies. Childeric king at Amiens	i.	12

A.D.		CHAP.	SECT.
466.	Clovis born	ii.	83
476.	Roman Empire in Italy ended by Odoacer	i.	12
481.	Roman Empire ended in France	ii.	83
	Clovis crowned at Amiens	{ i. ii.	12 2
	St. Benedict born	ii.	3
485.	Battle of Soissons. Clovis defeats Syagrius	ii.	83
486.	Syagrius dies at the court of Alaric	ii.	83
489.	Battle of Verona. Theodoric defeats Odoacer	ii.	88
493.	Clovis marries Clotilda	ii.	84
496.	Battle of Tolbiac. Clovis defeats the Alemanni	ii.	86
	Clovis crowned at Rheims by St. Rémy	i.	13
	Clovis baptized by St. Rémy	i.	20
508.	Battle of Poitiers. Clovis defeats the Visigoths under Alaric. Death of Alaric	i.	13

APPENDIX II.

REFERENCES EXPLANATORY OF THE PHOTO-GRAPHS ILLUSTRATING CHAPTER IV.

THE quatrefoils on the foundation of the west front of Amiens Cathedral, described in the course of the fourth chapter, had never been engraved or photographed in any form accessible to the public until last year, when I commissioned M. Kaltenbacher (6, Passage du Commerce), who had photographed them for M. Viollet le Duc, to obtain negatives of the entire series, with the central pedestal of the Christ.

The proofs are entirely satisfactory to me, and extremely honourable to M. Kaltenbacher's skill: and it is impossible to obtain any more instructive and interesting, in exposition of the manner of central thirteenth-century sculpture.

I directed their setting so that the entire succession of the quatrefoils might be included in eighteen plates; the front and two sides of the pedestal raise their number to twenty-one: the whole, unmounted, sold by my agent Mr. Ward (the negatives being my own property) for four guineas; or separately, each five shillings.

Besides these of my own, I have chosen four general views of the cathedral from M. Kaltenbacher's formerly-taken negatives, which, together with the first-named series, (twenty-five altogether,) will form a complete body of illustrations for the fourth chapter of the 'BIBLE OF AMIENS'; costing in all five guineas, forwarded free by post from Mr. Ward's (2, Church Terrace, Richmond, Surrey). In addition to these, Mr. Ward will supply the photograph of the four scenes from the life of St. Firmin, mentioned in Chapter I. § 7; price five shillings.*

For those who do not care to purchase the whole series, I have marked with an asterisk the plates which are especially desirable.

The two following lists will enable readers who possess the plates to refer without difficulty both from the photographs to the text, and from the text to the photographs, which will be found to fall into the following groups :—

Photographs.
    1–3. THE CENTRAL PEDESTAL.
        DAVID.
    4–7. THE CENTRAL PORCH.
        VIRTUES AND VICES.

---

* This is the first of another series of photographs illustrative of the cathedral, which has not been continued.—ED. (1897).

Photographs.

8–9. THE CENTRAL PORCH.
>THE MAJOR PROPHETS, WITH MICAH AND NAHUM.

10–13. THE FAÇADE.
>THE MINOR PROPHETS.

14–17. THE NORTHERN PORCH.
>THE MONTHS AND ZODIACAL SIGNS, WITH ZEPHANIAH AND HAGGAI.

18–21. THE SOUTHERN PORCH.
>SCRIPTURAL HISTORY, WITH OBADIAH AND AMOS.

22–25. MISCELLANEOUS.

PART I.

LIST OF PHOTOGRAPHS WITH REFERENCE TO THE QUATREFOILS, ETC.*

1–3. CENTRAL PEDESTAL. See §§ 32–33.

*1. FRONT . . . David. Lion and Dragon. Vine.
*2. NORTH SIDE . Lily and Cockatrice.
*3. SOUTH SIDE . . Rose and Adder.

4–7. CENTRAL PORCH.

Virtues and Vices (§§ 39 & 41).

4. 1 A. Courage.   2 A. Patience.   3 A. Gentillesse.
    1 B. Cowardice. 2 B. Anger.   3 B. Churlishness.

---

* The sections referred to in this Appendix are those of Chapter IV.—ED. (1897).

Photographs.

5.	4 A. Love.	5 A. Obedience.	6 A. Perseverance.
	4 B. Discord.	5 B. Rebellion.	6 B. Atheism.
6.	9 A. Charity.	8 A. Hope.	7 A. Faith.
	9 B. Avarice.	8 B. Despair.	7 B. Idolatry.
7	12 A. Humility.	11 A. Wisdom.	10 A. Chastity.
	12 B. Pride.	11 B. Folly.	10 B. Lust.

8–9. CENTRAL PORCH.

The Major Prophets (§§ 39, 42), with Micah and Nahum (§§ 40, 43).

*8	ISAIAH.	JEREMIAH.	MICAH.
	13 A.	14 A.	22 C.
	13 B.	14 B.	22 D.
9.	NAHUM.	DANIEL.	EZEKIEL.
	23 A.	16 A.	15 A.
	23 B.	16 B.	15 B.

10–13. THE FAÇADE.

The Minor Prophets (§§ 40, 43).

*10.	AMOS.	JOEL.	HOSEA.
	19 A.	18 A.	17 A.
	19 B.	18 B.	17 B.
*11.	MICAH.	JONAH.	OBADIAH.
	22 A.	21 A.	20 C.
	22 B.	21 B.	20 D.
*12.	ZEPHANIAH.	HABAKKUK.	NAHUM.
	25 A.	24 A.	23 C.
	25 B.	24 B.	23 D.
13.	MALACHI.	ZECHARIAH.	HAGGAI.
	28 A.	27 A.	26 C.
	28 B.	27 B.	26 D.

Photographs.

14–17. The Northern Porch.

The Months and Zodiacal Signs (§ 47), with Zephaniah and Haggai (§§ 40, 43).

	41.	42.	43.	44.
14.	Capricorn.	Aquarius.	Pisces.	Aries.
	December.	January.	February.	March.

	45.	46.	25 C.
15.	Taurus.	Gemini.	Zephaniah.
	April.	May.	25 D.

	26 A.	52.	51.
16.	Haggai.	Cancer.	Leo.
	26 B.	June.	July.

	50.	49.	48.	47.
17.	Virgo.	Libra.	Scorpio.	Sagittarius.
	August.	September.	October.	November.

18–21. The Southern Porch.

Scriptural History (§ 51), with Obadiah and Amos (§§ 40, 42, 43).

*18.   29 A. Daniel and the stone.   30 A. Gideon and the fleece.
29 B. Moses and the Burning Bush.   30 B. Moses and Aaron.
31 A. The message to Zacharias.   32 A. The silence of Zacharias.
31 B. Dream of Joseph.   32 B. "His name is John."

19.   33 A. The Flight into Egypt.   34 A. The Fall of the Idols.   19 C. Amos.
33 B. Christ and the Doctors.   34 B. Return to Nazareth.   19 D. Amos.

Photographs.

20.
- 20 A. Obadiah.
- 20 B. Obadiah.
- 40 A. Solomon and the Queen of Sheba. The Grace Cup.
- 40 B. Solomon teaching the Queen of Sheba. "God is above."
- 39 A. Solomon enthroned.
- 39 B. Solomon in prayer.

21.
- 38 A. Holy Innocents.
- 38 B. Herod orders the Kings' ship to be burnt.
- 36 A. Adoration in Bethlehem (?)
- 36 B. The voyage of the Kings.
- 37 A. Herod and the Kings.
- 37 B. The burning of the ship.
- 35 A. The Star in the East.
- 35 B. The Kings warned in a dream.

22-25. MISCELLANEOUS.

*22. THE WESTERN PORCHES.

*23. THE PORCH OF ST. HONORÉ.

24. THE SOUTH TRANSEPT AND FLÈCHE.

25. GENERAL VIEW OF THE CATHEDRAL FROM THE OTHER BANK OF THE SOMME.

PART II.

LIST OF QUATREFOILS WITH REFERENCE TO THE PHOTOGRAPHS.

Black letter No. in text.	Name of Statue.	Subject of Quatrefoil.	Section where described (chap. iv.)	No. of Photograph.
	The Apostles.	*Virtues and Vices.*		
1.	St. Peter	A. Courage B. Cowardice	§ 39 § 41 ,,	
2.	St. Andrew	A. Patience B. Anger	§ 39 § 41 ,,	4
3.	St. James	A. Gentillesse B. Churlishness	,, ,,	
4.	St. John	A. Love B. Discord	,, § 39 § 41	
5.	St. Matthew	A. Obedience B. Rebellion	§ 39 § 41 ,,	5
6.	St. Simon	A. Perseverance B. Atheism	,, § 39 § 41	
7.	St. Paul	A. Faith B. Idolatry	,, ,,	
8.	St. James the Bishop	A. Hope B. Despair	§ 39 § 41 ,,	6
9.	St. Philip	A. Charity B. Avarice	,, § 39 § 41	

Black letter No. in text.	Name of Statue.	Subject of Quatrefoil.	Section where described (chap. iv.)	No. of Photograph.
10.	St. Bartholomew	A. Chastity B. Lust	§ 41 ,,	7
11.	St. Thomas	A. Wisdom B. Folly	,, ,,	
12.	St. Jude	A. Humility B. Pride	§ 39 § 41 ,,	

The Major Prophets.

13.	Isaiah	A. The Lord enthroned B. Lo! this hath touched thy lips	§ 39 § 42	8
14.	Jeremiah	A. The burial of the girdle B. The breaking of the yoke	§ 39 § 42	
15.	Ezekiel	A. Wheel within wheel B. Set thy face towards Jerusalem	,, ,,	9
16.	Daniel	A. He hath shut the lions' mouths B. Fingers of a man's hand	,, § 39 § 42	

The Minor Prophets.

17.	Hosea	A. So I bought her to me B. So will I also be for thee	§ 40 § 43 § 40 § 43	10

Black letter No. in text.	Name of Statue.		Subject of Quatrefoil.	Section where described (chap. iv.)	No. of Photograph.
18.	JOEL		A. The sun and moon lightless . . .	§ 40 § 43	
			B. The fig-tree and vine leafless . .	,,	} 10
19.	AMOS	Façade	A. The Lord will cry from Zion . . .	,,	
			B. The habitations of the shepherds .	,,	
		Porch	C. The Lord with the mason's line . .	§ 40	} 19
			D. The place where it rained not . .	§ 43	
20.	OBADIAH	Porch	A. I hid them in a cave	,,	} 20
			B. He fell on his face	,,	
		Façade	C. The captain of fifty	,,	} 11
			D. The messenger .	,,	
21.	JONAH		A. Escaped from the sea	§ 43 § 40	
			B. Under the gourd .	§ 43	} 11
22.	MICAH	Façade	A. The tower of the Flock	,,	
			B. Each shall rest . .	,,	
		Porch	C. Swords into ploughshares	§ 40	} 8
			D. Spears into pruning-hooks. . .	§ 43	
23.	NAHUM	Porch	A. None shall look back	,,	} 9
			B. The Burden of Nineveh . . .	,,	
		Façade	C. Thy Princes and great ones . .	§ 40 § 43	
			D. Untimely figs . .	,,	} 12
24.	HABAKKUK		A. I will watch . . .	,,	
			B. The ministry to Daniel. . . .	,,	

Black letter No. in text.	Name of Statue.		Subject of Quatrefoil.	Section where described (chap. iv.)	No. of Photograph.
25. ZEPHANIAH.	Façade	A.	The Lord strikes Ethiopia	§ 40 § 43	12
		B.	The beasts in Nineveh	,,	
	Porch	C.	The Lord visits Jerusalem	,,	15
		D.	The Hedgehog and Bittern	,,	
26. HAGGAI	Porch	A.	The houses of the princes	§ 40	16
		B.	The Heaven stayed from dew	§ 43	
	Façade	C.	The temple desolate	,,	
		D.	Thus saith the Lord	,,	
27. ZECHARIAH		A.	The lifting up of Iniquity	,,	13
		B.	The angel that spake to me	,,	
28. MALACHI		A.	Ye have wounded the Lord	§ 40 § 43	
		B.	This commandment is to *you*	,,	

SOUTHERN PORCH—*to the Virgin.*

29. GABRIEL		A.	Daniel and the stone cut without hands	§ 51	
		B.	Moses and the burning bush	,,	
30. VIRGIN ANNUNCIATE		A.	Gideon and the fleece	,,	13
		B.	Moses and the law. Aaron and his rod	,,	
31. VIRGIN VISITANT		A.	The message to Zacharias	,,	
		B.	The dream of Joseph	,,	

Black letter No. in text.	Name of Statue.	Subject of Quatrefoil.	Section where described (chap. iv.)	No. of Photograph.
32.	ST. ELIZABETH.	A. The silence of Zacharias B. "His name is John".	§ 51 ,,	13
33.	VIRGIN IN PRESENTATION.	A. Flight into Egypt. B. Christ with the Doctors.	,, ,,	19
34.	ST. SIMEON	A. Fall of Idols in Egypt. B. The return to Nazareth.	,, ,,	
35.	THE FIRST KING.	A. The Star in the East. B. "Warned in a dream".	,, ,,	
36.	THE SECOND KING	A. Adoration in Bethlehem (?). B. The voyage of the Kings.	,, ,,	21
37.	THE THIRD KING	A. Herod inquires of the Kings. B. The burning of the ship.	,, ,,	
38.	HEROD	A. Massacre of the Innocents. B. Herod orders the ship to be burnt.	,, ,,	
39.	SOLOMON.	A. Solomon enthroned B. Solomon in prayer	,, ,,	20
40.	QUEEN OF SHEBA.	A. The Grace cup. B. "God is above".	,, ,,	

NORTHERN PORCH—*to St. Firmin* (p. 234, § 44).

| 41. | ST. FIRMIN CONFESSOR | A. Capricorn
B. December | § 47
,, | 14 |

Black letter No. in text.	Name of Statue.	Subject of Quatrefoil.	Section where described (chap. iv.)	No. of Photograph.
42.	St. Domice	A. Aquarius B. January	§ 47 ,,	
43.	St. Honoré	A. Pisces B. February	,, ,,	14
44.	St. Salve	A. Aries B. March	,, ,,	
45.	St. Quentin	A. Taurus B. April	,, ,,	
46.	St. Gentian	A. Gemini B. May	,, ,,	15
47.	St. Geoffroy	A. Sagittarius B. November	,, ,,	
48.	An Angel	A. Scorpio B. October	,, ,,	
49.	St. Fuscien, Martyr	A. Libra B. September	,, ,,	17
50.	St. Victoric, Martyr	A. Virgo B. August	,, ,,	
51.	An Angel	A. Leo B. July	,, ,,	
52.	St. Ulpha	A. Cancer B. June	,, ,,	16

APPENDIX III.

GENERAL PLAN OF 'OUR FATHERS HAVE TOLD US.' *

THE first part of 'Our Fathers have told us,' now submitted to the public, is enough to show the proposed character and tendencies of the work, to which, contrary to my usual custom, I now invite subscription, because the degree in which I can increase its usefulness by engraved illustration must greatly depend on the known number of its supporters.

I do not recognize, in the present state of my health, any reason to fear more loss of general power, whether in conception or industry, than is the proper and appointed check of an old man's enthusiasm: of which, however, enough remains in me to warrant my readers against the abandonment of a purpose entertained already for twenty years.

The work, if I live to complete it, will consist of ten parts, each taking up some local division of

* Reprinted from the "Advice," issued with Chap. III. (March, 1882).

Christian history, and gathering, towards their close, into united illustration of the power of the Church in the Thirteenth Century.

The present volume completes the first part, descriptive of the early Frank power, and of its final skill, in the Cathedral of Amiens.

The second part, "Ponte della Pietra," will, I hope, do more for Theodoric and Verona than I have been able to do for Clovis and the first capital of France.

The third, "Ara Celi," will trace the foundations of the Papal power.

The fourth, "Ponte-a-Mare," and fifth, "Ponte Vecchio," will only with much difficulty gather into brief form what I have by me of scattered materials respecting Pisa and Florence.

The sixth, "Valle Crucis," will be occupied with the monastic architecture of England and Wales.

The seventh, "The Springs of Eure," will be wholly given to the cathedral of Chartres.

The eighth, "Domrémy," to that of Rouen and the schools of architecture which it represents.

The ninth, "The Bay of Uri," to the Pastoral forms of Catholicism, reaching to our own times.

And the tenth, "The Bells of Cluse," to the pastoral Protestantism of Savoy, Geneva, and the Scottish border.

Each part will consist of four sections only; and one of them, the fourth, will usually be descriptive of some monumental city or cathedral, the resultant and remnant of the religious power examined in the preparatory chapters.

One illustration at least will be given with each chapter, and drawings made for others, which will be placed at once in the Sheffield museum for public reference, and engraved as I find support, or opportunity for binding with the completed work.

As in the instance of Chapter IV. of this first part, a smaller edition of the descriptive chapters will commonly be printed in reduced form for travellers and non-subscribers ; but otherwise, I intend this work to be furnished to subscribers only.

INDEX.

INDEX.

[*The references in this index are to the sections of each chapter. Thus iv. 51 is to Chapter* IV., § 51.]

AARON'S rod, iv. 51.
Adder, the deaf, iv. 33-34.
Admiration, test of, iv. 8.
Afghan war, ii. 43.
Agricola, iii. 21.
Aisles of aspen and of stone, iv. 10.
Alaric (son-in-law of Theodoric), defeated and killed by Clovis at Poitiers, i. 14; ii. 49.
  ,, the younger, ii. 49.
Albofleda, sister of Clovis, ii. 48.
Alemannia (Germany), ii. 19.
Alexander III. and Barbarossa, iv. 35.
Alfred, King, of England, religious feeling under, i. 34 *n*.
Algeria, iii. 13.
Alphabet, the, and Mœsia, iii. 22.
Alps, the, and climbing, iii. 29.
Amiens. (1) History; (2) Town; (3) Cathedral.
  (1) *History of:*—
      early people of, and Roman gods, i. 6.
      taken by the Franks under Clodion, 445 A.D., i. 10.
      manufactures of, early, i. 2, 3.
          ,,   swords, iv. 43.
          ,,   woollen, i. 186; iv. 41.
      religion, and Christianity :—
          the Beau Christ d'Amiens, iv. 3, 36.

Amiens, (1) *History of (continued)* :—
    S. Firmin the first to preach there, 300 A.D., i. 6, 7 seqq.
    the first bishopric of France, i. 8.
    the first church there, 350 A.D., i. 8, 9; iv. 14.
    under St. Geoffroy, 1104-50 A.D., iv. 45.
(2) *The Town* :—
    country round, i. 3.
    highest land near, i. 22.
    manufactory chimneys, i. 4, 8.
    railway station, i. 1, 4.
    Roman gate near, i. 22.
    St. Acheul, chimney of, i. 8, 22.
    streams and rivers of, i. 2.
    the "Venice of France," i. 2.
3) *The Cathedral* :—
  (*a*) History ;—
    books on, iv. 5 *n*.
    building of, iv. 2.
      ,, by whom? iv. 12.
    completion of, rhyme on the, iv. 12.
    history of successive churches on its site, iv. 14.
  (*b*) General aspect of ;—
    as compared with other cathedrals, iv. 1.
    the consummation of Frankish character, ii. 38.
    the "Parthenon of Gothic architecture," iv. 1.
  (*c*) Detailed examination of ;—
    approaches to, which best, iv. 6.
    apse, the, its height, iv. 9.
      ,, the first perfect piece of Northern architecture, iv. 11.
    choir, the, and wood-carving, iv. 5 and *n*.
    façade, iv. 28 seq.
      ,, the central porch ;—
      ,,   ,, apostles of, iv. 29.
      ,,   ,, Christ-Immanuel, David, iv. 28.
      ,,   ,, prophets of, iv. 29.
      ,, the northern porch (St. Firmin), iv. 44.
      ,, the southern porch (Madonna), iv. 48.
    flèche, from station, i. 4, 5 ; iv. 7, 58.
    foundation steps, the old, removed, iv. 27.

Amiens, (3) *The Cathedral (continued)* :—
        restoration of, iv. 27, 43.
        rose moulding of, iv. 27.
        sculptures of, iv. 51.
           ,,   of prophets better than of virtues, iv. 42.
        transepts of ; North, rose window, iv. 8.
           ,,   ,,   sculpture of, iv. 43 *n*.
           ,,   South, Madonna on, iv. 7.
Amos, figure and quatrefoils, Amiens Cathedral, iv. 43.
Anchorites, early, iii. 29, 30.
Anderson, J. R., on purgatory, iv. 55 *n*.
Angelico, scriptural teaching of, iii. 46.
Anger, bides its time, iii. 42.
   ,, a feminine vice, iv. 41.
   ,, sculpture of, Amiens Cathedral, iv. 41.
Angoulême, legend of its walls falling, ii. 47 *n*.
Aphrodite, ii. 3.
Apocrypha, the, received by the Church, iii. 40.
Apostles, the, and virtues, Amiens Cathedral, iv. 37 seq.
Arab, Gothic and Classic, iii. 13.
Arabia, iii. 13.
   ,, power and religion of, iii. 19.
   ,, Sir F. Palgrave's book on, iii. 17-18.
Architecture, Egyptian, origin of, iii. 27.
      ,,   literal character of early Christian, iv. 4.
      ,,   and nature, iv. 10.
      ,,   Northern, gets as much light as possible, i. 139; iv. 2.
      ,,   ,, passion of, iv. 10.
      ,,   "purity of style" in, iv. 2.
Arianism of Visigoths, i. 13.
Arles, defeat of Clovis by Theodoric at, ii. 47, 53.
Armour, early Frankish, ii. 33.
Art, the Bible as influencing and influenced by Christian, iii. 45-46.
  ,, all great, praise, pref. iv.
  ,, and literature, mental action of, iii. 47.
Asceticism, our power of rightly estimating, iii. 29.
Asia, seven churches of, iii. 12.
  ,, Minor, a misnomer, iii. 12.
  ,, religious feeling of Asiatics, i. 35.

Assyria, ancient kingdom of, and the Jews, iii. 18.
Astronomy from Egypt, iii. 27.
Atheism, barefoot figure of, Amiens Cathedral, iv. 41.
  ,,   wise men may be idolaters, cannot be atheists, iv. 41.
  ,,   modern: see s. "Infidelity."
Athena, iii. 53.
Athens, influence of, on Europe, iii. 12.
Atlantic cable, iii. 8.
Attila, defeated at Chalons, i. 10.
Attuarii, ii. 18, 28 n.
Augurs, college of, iii. 26 n.
Aurelian, the Emperor, a Dacian, ii. 15.
Auroch herds, of Scythia, ii. 11.
Author, the :—
  (a). *Generally :*—
    art teaching of, iii. 52.
    Bible training of, iii. 52.
    on his own books, iii. 52.
    cathedrals, his love of, iv. 1.
    conservative, pref. i.
    discursiveness of, ii. 40.
    on Greek myths, iii. 52.
    on Homer and Horace, iii. 52.
    religion of, iv. 55 seq.
    on Roman religion, iii. 52.
    travels abroad; earliest tour on Continent, iv. 13.
      ,,   at Amiens, in early life, iv. 27.
      ,,   at Avallon, Aug 28, '82, iii. 54.
  (b). *Books of, quoted or referred to :*—
    Ariadne Florentina, on "franchise," ii. 28.
    Arrows of the Chace, letters to Glasgow, pref. i.
    Fiction Fair and Foul, iv. 35 n.
    Fors Clavigera, Letter 61 (Vol. V., p. 22), iv. 20 n.
      ,,   ,,   ,, 65 (Vol. VI., p. 157), iv. 43 n.
    Laws of Fésolé, pref. iv; iii. 7.
    Modern Painters, plate 73, i. 31.
    St. Mark's Rest, ii. 42; iii. 48 n.; iv. 36.
    Stones of Venice, iv. 49 n.
    Two Paths, iv. 8 n.
    Val d'Arno, ii. 28 n.

INDEX.

Auvergnats, i. 16.
Avarice, modern, iv. 35, 41.
   ,,   figure of, Amiens Cathedral, iv. 41.

BACTERIA, the, i. 19.
Baltic, tribes of the, ii. 11, 12.
Baptism, not essential to salvation, i. 29.
Barbarossa, in the porch of St. Mark's, iv. 35.
Batavians, ii. 45.
Battle-axe, French, or Achon, ii. 32.
Bayeux, Bishop of, Earl of Salisbury's surrender to, iv. 24
Beauvais, Cathedral of, iv. 1.
Beggars, how to give to, iv. 8.
Belshazzar's feast, iv. 42.
" Bible of Amiens," meaning of title, iv. 44.
Bible, the Holy—
  ,,   art, as influenced by, iii. 45.
  ,,   and Clovis, ii. 47.
  ,,   contents and matchless compass of, iii. 51.
  ,,   disobedience of accepting only what we like in it, iii. 41.
  ,,   history of, and acceptance by the Church, iv. 39, 40.
  ,,   influence of, sentimental, intellectual, moral, iii. 42.
  ,,   inspiration of the, iii. 48.
  ,,   the " library of Europe," iii. 36.
  ,,   literature and, iii. 44.
  ,,   St. Jerome's, iii. 26.
  ,,   study of, by the author as a child, iii. 52.
  ,,   ,,   honest and dishonest, iii. 42.
  ,,   ,,   one-sided, and its results, iii. 41.
  ,,   teaching of, general and special, iii. 49.
  ,,   Ulphilas' Gothic, iii. 22.
  ,,   the word ' Bible,' its meaning, iii. 37.
Bible, quoted or referred to :—*

    Gen. xviii. 25.   Shall not the Judge of all the earth do right? iv. 60.
    Exodus xiv. 15.   Speak unto the children of Israel, that they go forward, iv. 21 n.

---

* References merely descriptive of one of the sculptures of the façade of Amiens Cathedral are omitted in this index.

Bible, quoted or referred to (*continued*) :—

Deut. xxvi. 5.	A Syrian ready to perish was my father, iii. 14.
1 Sam. xvii. 28.	With whom hast thou left those few sheep in the wilderness? iii. 26.
Ps. xi. 4.	The Lord is in His holy temple, iv. 2.
Ps. xiv. 1.	The fool hath said (*Dixit insipiens*), iv. 41.
Ps. xxiv.	Who is the King of Glory? iv. 36.
Ps. lxv. 12.	The little hills rejoice on every side, iv. 60.
Song of Sol. vii. 1.	How beautiful are thy feet with shoes, iv. 41.
Isa. xi. 9.	Hurt nor destroy in all the holy mountain, iv. 54.
Matt. x. 37.	He that loveth father or mother more than Me, iii. 36.
,, xvi. 24.	Let him take up his cross and follow Me. iii. 43.
,, xvii. 5.	This is My beloved Son . . . hear ye Him, iv. 30.
,, xviii. 20.	Where two or three are gathered together, iv. 3.
,, xxi. 9.	Hosanna to the Son of David, iv. 31.
Luke i. 80.	The child grew . . . and was in the deserts, iii. 26.
,, x. 5.	Peace be to this house, iv. 38.
,, x. 28.	This do, and thou shalt live, iv. 54.
,, xvi. 31.	If they hear not Moses and the prophets, iii. 38.
John vi. 29.	This is the work of God, that ye believe Him, i. 4.
,, vi. 55.	Except ye eat the flesh of the Son of man, iv. 41.
,, xvii. 23.	I in them, and thou in Me, iv. 41.
,, xxi. 16.	Feed my sheep, iv. 26.
Rom. viii. 4, 6, 13.	The righteousness of the law . . . for to be carnally minded is death, iii. 48 *n.*
1 Cor. xiii 6.	Rejoiceth not in iniquity, but in the truth, pref. iv.
2 Cor. vi. 16.	I will be their God and they shall be My people, iv. 3.
Eph. iv. 26.	Let not the sun go down upon your wrath, iii. 42.
,, vi. 15.	Your feet shod with the preparation of the gospel of peace, iv. 41.
James v. 7, 8.	Be ye also patient, iv. 41.
Rev. iii. 11.	Hold fast that which thou hast, iv. 41.
,, xi. 15.	The kingdoms of this world are become the kingdoms of our Lord, and of His Christ, iv. 60.

Bibliotheca, iii. 37.
Bishops, French, in battle, iv. 24. See s. Everard and St. Geoffroy.
Bittern and nedgehog, iv. 43.
Black's atlas, ii. 24.
Black Prince, the, his leopard coinage, iv. 41.
,,   ,,   ,, at Limoges, iv. 41.
Blasphemy and slang, iv. 25.
Blight, as a type of punishment, iv. 43.
Boden see, the, ii. 25.
Boulin, Arnold, carves choir of Amiens Cathedral, iv. 5.
Bourges, Cathedral of, iv. 1.
Bouvines, battle of, iv. 24.
Bretons, in France, i. 9, 12, 16.
Britain, gives Christianity its first deeds and final legends, ii. 15.
,, divisions of, iii. 24.
,, and Roman Empire, ii. 9.
Brocken summit, the, ii. 22.
Bructeri, ii. 18.
Bunyan, John, i. 25.
Burgundy, and France distinct, i. 9, 12, 16.
,, extent of kingdom, *temp.* Clotilde, ii. 49.
,, king of, uncle of Clotilde, ii. 50.
Bussey and Gaspey's History of France, ii. 50.
Butler, Colonel, "Far out: Rovings retold," pref. ii., i. 35 *n*.
Byron's "Cain," iii. 44.
Byzantine Madonna, iv. 49.
,, scheme of the Virtues, iv. 36.
Byzantium, influence of, on Europe, iii. 12.

CALAIS, road from, to Paris, i. 16.
Callousness of modern public opinion, ii. 42.
Camels, disobedient and ill-tempered, iv. 41.
Canary Islands, iii. 13.
Cancan, the, iv. 41.
Canterbury, St. Martin's church at, and St. Augustine, i. 29.
Canute, iii. 16.
Carlyle, T., description of Poland and Prussia, ii. 10.
,, "Frederick the Great" quoted, iii. 47.
Carpaccio, draperies in the pictures of, i. 2 *n*.
Carthage, iii. 13.

Cary's Dante, iv. 36 n., 41.   See s. Dante.
Cassel, ii. 24.
Cathedrals, author's love of, iv. 1.
    ,,   custodians of, iv. 1.
    ,,   different, French and English, compared with that of Amiens, iv. 1.
    ,,   plan of mediæval, and its religious meaning, iv. 4.
    ,,   points of compass in, iv. 28.
Catti, the, ii. 18, 27.
Cattle, huge, of nomad tribes, ii. 11.
Centuries, division of the, into four periods, ii. 1.
Chalons, defeat of Attila at, i. 10.
Chamavi, ii. 18.
Chapman, George, his last prayer, iv. 20-21.
Charity, giving to beggars, iv. 8.
    ,,   indiscriminate, iv. 41.
Charlemagne, religion under, i. 34 n.
Chartres Cathedral, iv. 1.
Chastity, Amiens Cathedral, iv. 41.
Chaucer, " Romaunt of Rose" quoted on franchise, ii. 28 n.
Chauci, ii. 18, 27.
Childebert (son of Clovis), first Frank king of Paris, ii. 48.
    ,,   meaning of the word, ii. 48.
Childeric, son of Merovée, King of Franks, exiled 457 A.D., i. 10.
Chivalry, its dawn and darkening, ii. 33.
    ,,   its Egyptian origin, iii. 27.
    ,,   feudal, ii. 54.
Chlodomir, second son of Clovis, ii. 48.
Chlodowald, son of Chlodomir, ii. 48.
Christ, the Beau Christ d'Amiens, iv. 3, 36.
    ,,   and the doctors, iv. 51.
    ,,   His life, not His death, to be mainly contemplated, iv. 52.
    ,,   His return to Nazareth, iv. 51.
    ,,   realization of His presence by mediæval burghers, iv. 3.
    ,,   statue of, Amiens Cathedral, iv. 28, 36.
    ,,   ,,   ,,   ,,   its meaning, &c., iv. 52.
Christian, The (newspaper), iii. 48.
Christianity and the Bible, iii. 26.
    ,,   of Clovis, i. 21.
    ,,   early, share of Britain, Gaul and Germany in, ii. 15.

Christianity, fifth century, at end of, ii. 54.
,,   Gentile, iii. 39.
,,   Gothic, Classic, Arab, iii. 25.
,,   literature as influencing, iii. 26.
,,   mediæval, Saxon and Frank, i. 34, 35.
,,   modern, i. 27.
,,   modest minds, the best recipients of, iii. 39.
,,   monastic life, iii. 26.
,,   St. Jerome's Bible, and, iii. 37.
,,   true, defined, iv. 55, 57.
,,   See s. Religion.

Church, the first French, at Amiens, i. 8.
Churlishness, figure of, Amiens Cathedral, iv. 41.
Cimabue's Madonna, iv. 49.
Cincinnatus, iii. 21.
Circumstances, man the creature of, iii. 1, 3.
Classic countries of Europe (Gothic and Arab), iii. 11.
,,   literature, there is a *sacred*, iii. 53.
Claudius, the Emperor, a Dacian, ii. 15.
Clergymen, modern, i. 27.
,,   Protestant, iii. 33.
Climate, and nationality, i. 15.
,,   races divided by, iii. 9.
,,   and race, their influence on man, iii. 9.
Cloak, legend of St. Martin's, i. 22-23.
Clodion, leads Franks over Rhine, takes Amiens, 445 A.D., i. 10.
Clotaire, son of Clovis, ii. 48.
Clotilde (wife of Clovis, daughter of Chilperic), i. 9, 34.
,,   education of, ii. 49.
,,   the god of, i. 9, 13, 21.
,,   ,,   ii. 54.
,,   journeys to France, ii. 50.
,,   marriage of, i. 13; ii. 48.
,,   mother of, ii. 49 *n*.
,,   name, meaning of the, ii. 48.
———   (daughter of Clovis and Clotilde), ii. 48.
Clovis, King of the Franks, i. 9.
,,   birth of, 466 A.D., ii. 49.
,,   character of, i. 21.

Clovis, death and last years of, ii. 44.
,, family of, ii. 48.
,, name, meaning of the, ii. 48.
,, reign of, i. 20.
,, crowned at Amiens, 481 A.D., ii. 2.
,, ,, at Rheims, i. 13.
,, defeat of, by Ostrogoths, at Arles, ii. 47.
,, passes the Loire, at Tours, i. 33.
,, and the Soissons vase, ii. 41-43.
,, summary of its events, ii. 49.
,, victories of (Soissons, Poitiers, Tolbiac,) i. 13, 34 *n*.
,, ,, the Franks after his, ii. 38.
,, religion of :—
,, prays to the God of Clotilde, i. 9, 13, 21 ; ii. 54.
,, conversion to Christianity by St. Remy, i. 20-21.
,, his previous respect for Christianity, ii. 49 *n*.
,, ,, ,, St. Martin's Abbey, i. 32.
,, his Christianity, analysed, ii. 47.
,, Rheims enriched by, ii. 49.
,, St. Genevieve, Paris, founded by, ii. 55.
——— son of Childeric, i. 11.
,, ,, ,, invades Italy, ii. 28 *n*.
,, ,, ,, reign of, i. 10.
Cockatrice, sculpture of the, Amiens Cathedral, iv. 33-34.
Cockneyism, history-writing and, i. 21.
,, 'Mossoo,' ii. 27.
,, priests and, iv. 41.
Coinage, the Black Prince's leopard, iv. 41.
Colchos, tribes of the lake of, ii. 11.
Cologne, battlefield of Tolbiac from, ii. 54.
Commerce and Protestantism, iii. 43.
Competition will not produce art, iv. 4 *n*.
,, ,, and the Franks, ii. 31 *n*.
Constantine, Emperor, power of, ii. 54.
,, ,, lascivious court of, iii. 20.
Constantius, Emperor, a Dacian, ii. 15 *n*.
Courage, figure of, Amiens Cathedral, iv. 41.
Covetousness and atheism, iv. 41.
Cowardice, figure of, Amiens Cathedral, iv. 41.
Creasy, Sir E., "History of England," iii. 5, 6.

Crecy, battle of, Edward II. fords the Somme, i. 2.
Crime, the history of, its possible lessons, i. 18.
Cross, the power of the, in history, iii. 42.
  ,,   Protestant view of the, as a raft of salvation, iii. 43.
Crown, the, of Hope, iv. 41.
Cyrene, iii. 13.

DACIA, contest of, with Rome, ii. 9.
  ,,   five Roman emperors from, ii. 15 *n*.
Dædalus, iv. 19.
Dalmatia, iii. 23.
Danes, the, ii. 12.
Daniel, statue, etc., of, Amiens Cathedral, iv. 38, 42.
        quatrefoils: 'traditional visit of Habakkuk to,' iv. 43.
          ,,   the stone cut without hands, iv. 51.
Dante, as a result of the Bible, iii. 44.
  ,,   Christian-heathen poet, iv. 20.
  ,,   Virgil's influence on, iii. 53.
  ,,   quoted: "Paradise" (28), iv. 36 *n*.
  ,,   ,,   ,,   (125), iv. 41.
Danube, tribes of the, ii. 11.
Darwinism, ii. 30; iv. 43.
Dates, recollection of exact, ii. 1, 2, 17.
David and monastic life, iii. 26.
  ,,   statue of, Amiens Cathedral, iv. 31.
Dead, recognition of the, in a future life, iv. 60.
Denmark, under Canute, iii. 16.
Despair, figure of, Amiens Cathedral, iv. 41.
Devil, St. Martin's answer to the, i. 28.
Diocletian, retirement of, iii. 20.
Discipline, essential to man, iv. 29.
Dniester, importance of the, iii. 9-10.
Doctor, preaching at Matlock, iii. 48 *n*.
Douglas', Bishop, translation of Virgil, iii. 53; iv. 20.
Dove, the, a type of humility, iv. 41.
  ,,   ,, Isaac Walton's river, i. 2.
Dover cliff and parade, iv. 9.
Drachenfels, district of the, ii. 20, 22.
Dragon, under feet of the Christ, Amiens Cathedral, iv. 34.
Druids, in France, i. 6.

Durham Cathedral, iv. 1.
Dusevel's history of Amiens, i. 2 *n*.

EAST, geography of the, iii. 17, 18.
Eder, the, ii. 24.
Egypt, iii. 13.
,, Flight into, iv. 51.
,, Idols, the fall of, in, iv. 51.
,, influence of, iii. 19.
,, and the origin of learning, iii. 27.
,, theology of, and Greece, iii. 27.
Eisenach, ii. 24.
Elbe, tribes of the, ii. 11.
Elijah, figure of, Amiens Cathedral, iv. 43.
Engel-bach, ii. 24.
England, dominions of (story of C. Fox and Frenchman), iii. 5 6.
,, modern politics of: Afghan war, ii. 43.
,, ,, ,, Ireland, pref. i. 2 ; iii. 6.
,, ,, ,, Scotch crofters, iii. 6.
,, ,, ,, Zulu-land, ii. 43 ; iii. 6.
,, pride of wealth, iii. 7.
,, St. Germain comes to, ii. 5.
,, streams of (Croydon, Guildford, Winchester), i. 3.
English cathedrals, iv. 1.
,, character, stolid, French active, ii. 30.
,, language, its virtues, nobler than Latin, iv. 24.
,, tourist, the, iii. 29.
,, ,, the, initial-cutting by, iv. 12.
Ethiopia, the Lord striking, iv. 43.
Europe, condition and history of, 1–500 A.D., ii. 13, 54.
,, countries of, twelve, iii. 14.
,, division of, into Gothic and Classic, iii. 11 seq.
,, ,, by Vistula and Dniester, iii. 9-10.
,, geography of, iii. 9-18, 22-23 seq.
,, Greek part of, iii. 12.
,, ,, imagination, and Roman order, influence of, iii. 20.
,, nomad tribes of, ii. 11, and *n*.
,, peasant life of early, ii. 13.
Evangelical doctrine and commerce, iii. 43.

Everard, Bishop of Amiens, his tomb, iv. 24.
Executions, ancient and modern, ii. 43.
Ezekiel, figure of Amiens Cathedral, iv. 42.

FAITH, justification by, iv. 56.
,,   mediæval, iv. 3.
,,   sculpture of, Amiens Cathedral, iv. 41.
,,   "the substance of things hoped for," iv. 60.
,,   symbolism of, with cup and cross, iv. 41.
,,   and works, iv. 52 seq.
Fanaticism, and the Bible, iii. 41.
Fathers, the, Scriptural commentaries of, iii. 46.
,,   theology of the, iv. 55.
Faust, Goethe's, i. 7; ii. 21; iii. 44.
Favine, André (historian, 1620), on Frankish character, ii. 30, 32.
Feud, etymology of, iv. 17 *n*.
Florence, Duomo of, iv. 1.
Folly, sculpture of, Amiens Cathedral, iv. 41.
Fortitude, sculpture of, Amiens Cathedral, iv. 41.
Fox, Charles, his boast of England, iii. 5.
,, Dr., Quaker, preaching at Matlock, iii. 48 *n*.
France, Amiens and Calais, country between, i. 3.
,,   architecture of, no stone saw used, iv. 2 *n*.
,,   books on: Pictorial History of, i. 34; ii. 43.
,,   ,,   "Villes de France," ii. 50 *n*.
,,   cathedrals of, the, iv. 1.
      their outside "the wrong side of the stuff," iv. 8.
      restoration of, iv. 47.
,,   churches of, the first, at Amiens, i. 8.
,,   colours of the shield of, ii. 3.
,,   early tribes of, i. 8, 12.
,,   and the Franks, i. 9 seq.
,,   geography and geology of northern, i. 16.
,,   the Isle of, Paris, iv. 58.
,,   Kings of (Philip the Wise, Louis VIII., St. Louis), iv. 16.
,,   map of, showing early divisions, i. 12.
,,   Merovingian dynasty, i. 34.
,,   peoples of, divided by climates, i. 15.

T

France, provinces of, i. 16.
,, Prussia, war with, ii. 17.
,, rivers of, the five, i. 12.
See below, s. French.
Franchise, ii. 28 *n*.
Francisca (Frankish weapon), ii. 32.
Frank, meaning of, 'brave' rather than 'free,' ii. 27-28.
Frankenberg, ii. 24-25.
Frankness, meaning of, i. 9 ; ii. 28.
,, opposite of shyness, ii. 28 and *n*.
Franks, the, agriculture, sport, and trade of, ii. 37.
,, appearance of, ii. 34, 35.
,, character of, ii. 15, 35, 38.
,, etymology of word, ii. 32.
,, hair, manner of wearing the, by, ii. 36 ; iv. 43 *n*.
,, Holland and, ii. 30.
,, Julian defeats them, 358 A.D., ii. 31 *n*., 35.
,, Kings of the, i. 9 seqq.
,, modern, i. 34.
,, race of, originally German, ii. 15, 17, 24.
,, religion of, under St. Louis, i. 35.
,, rise of, 250 A.D., i. 9 seq.; ii. 17.
,, settled in France, *ib*.
extension of power, to the Loire, i. 13.
,, ,, to the Pyrenees, *ibid*.
,, Gaul becomes France, iii. 16.
,, the Rhine refortified against them, ii. 28 *n*., 31.
,, tribes of, Gibbon on the, ii. 18.
weapons of the, Achon and Francisca, ii. 32, 33.
French character, early, i. 11.
,, ,, its activity, ii. 29.
,, ,, its innate truth, ii. 16.
,, ,, its loyalty, "good subjects of a good king," ii. 29.
,, ,, makes perfect servants, ii. 28.
,, frogs, ii. 30.
,, liberty and activity, ii. 29.
,, ,, equality, and fraternity, under Clovis, ii. 42.
,, politeness, ii. 15.
,, religion, old and new, iv. 41.
,, Revolution, "They may eat grass," i. 33.

French Revolution, a revolt against lies, ii. 16.
,,   ,,   and irreligion, iv. 7, 23.
Froissart, quoted, ii. 33
Fulda, towns on the, ii. 24.
Future life, recognition of the dead in a, iv. 60.

GABRIEL, the Angel, figure of, Amiens Cathedral, iv. 50.
Gascons, the, not really French, i. 16.
Gauls, the, in France, i. 9.
    ,,   become French, iii. 16.
    ,,   meaning of the word, ii. 8 seqq.
    ,,   and Rome, ii. 9.
Gentillesse, figure of, Amiens Cathedral, iv. 41.
Geoffroy, Bishop, see s. S. Geoffroy.
Geometry, from Egypt, iii. 27.
Germany, Alemannia, ii. 19.
    ,,   and the Franks, i. 13; ii. 15 *n.*, 17.
    ,,   and Rome, ii. 9.
    ,,   domestic manners of, ii. 23.
    ,,   dukedoms of, small, ii. 19.
    ,,   geography of, ii. 20.
    ,,   geology of, ii. 25.
    ,,   maps of, ii. 19.
    ,,   mountains of, ii. 23.
    ,,   railroads of, ii. 19.
    ,,   S. Martin, and the Emperor of, i. 30.
    ,,   tribes, Germanic, ii. 18.
Gibbon's "Roman Empire." (*a*) its general character; (*b*) references to it.
   (*a*) its general character :—
           contempt for Christianity, ii. 44.
           its errors, iii. 29 *n.*
           inaccurate generalization, iii. 23-24 and *n.*
           its epithets always gratis, ii. 34.
           no fixed opinion on anything, ii. 31 *n.*
           not always consistent, ii. 38.
           satisfied moral serenity of, ii. 27.
           sneers of, ii. 48.
           style, rhetorical, ii. 35, 37; iii. 21.

Gibbon's "Roman Empire" (*continued*):—
 (*b*) references to, in present book :—
  on Angoulême, its walls falling (xxxviii. 53),* ii. 47.
  on asceticism (xxxvii. 72), iii. 29.
  Christianity (xv. 23, 33), iii. 39.
  Clovis (xxxviii. 17), ii. 45-46, 49.
  Egypt and monasticism (xxxvii. 6), iii. 27.
  Europe, divisions of (xxv.), iii. 23.
   ,, nations of (lvi.), iii. 19 *n*.
  Franks, the :—
   ,, their armour (xxxv. 18), ii. 34-35.
   ,, ,, aspect (xxxv. 18), ii. 36-38.
   ,, ,, character (xix. 79, 80), ii. 36-38.
   ,, ,, freemen (x. 73), ii. 31 *n*.
   ,, ,, rise (x. 69), ii. 17.
   ,, crossing the Rhine (xix. 64), ii. 31 *n*.
  after Tolbiac (xxxviii. 24), ii. 52.
  Gnostics (xv. 23, 33), iii. 39 *n*.
  Justinian (xl. 2), ii. 15 *n*.
  miracles (xxxviii. 53), ii. 47 *n*.
  monasticism (xxxvii.), iii. 26.
  monkish character (xxxvii. 72), iii. 29.
  Roman Empire and its divisions (xxv. 29), iii. 21-22.
  Scots and Celts (xxv. 109, 111), iii. 24 *n*.
  Theodobert's death (xli. 103), ii. 11 *n*.
  Theodoric, government of (xxxix. 43), ii. 53.
   ,, at Verona (xxxix. 19), ii. 54.
  Tolbiac, battle of (xxxviii. 24), ii. 52.
Gideon and the fleece, figure of, Amiens Cathedral, iv. 51.
Gilbert, Mons., on Amiens Cathedral, iv. 14.
 ,, ,, ,, bronze tombs in, iv. 23.
Ginevra and Imogen, ii. 3.
Giotto, scriptural teaching of, iii. 46.
Globe, divisions of the, iii. 8.
Gnostics, iii. 39.
God's kingdom in our hearts, i. 136 ; iii. 54.
Godfrey, see s. S. Geoffroy.

 * The references to Gibbon in this index are to the chapters of his history, together with the number of the note nearest to which the quotation occurs.

Gonfalon standard, the, iv. 41.
Gothic architecture, aim of a builder of, iv. 2.
  ,, cathedral, the five doors of a, iv. 28.
  ,, classic and Arab, iii. 19.
  ,, and Classic Europe, iii. 11.
  ,, wars with Rome, iii. 20.
Goths, the, see s. Ostrogoths, Visigoths.
Gourds, of Amiens, iv. 43.
Government, and nationality, iii. 15.
Goyer, Mons. (bookseller), Amiens, iv. 41.
Grass, pillage of, and Clovis, i. 32.
Greek, the alphabet how far, iii. 22.
  ,, all Europe south of Danube is, iii. 12, 22.
  ,, imagination in Europe, iii. 20.
  ,, myths and Christian legends, iii. 53.
Greeks, the, and Roman Empire, ii. 12.
Greta and Tees, ii. 24.
Guards, the Queen's (in Ireland, 1880), pref. i.
Guelph, etymology of, iv. 46.
Guinevere, ii. 3.

HABAKKUK, figure of, Amiens Cathedral, iv. 43.
Haggai, ,, ,, ,, iv. 43.
Hair, Frankish manner of wearing the, ii. 36; iv. 43 *n*.
Hartz mountains, ii. 20.
Hedgehog and bittern, iv. 43.
Heligoland, ii. 12.
Henry VIII. and the Pope, iv. 41.
Heraldry, English leopard from France, ii. 31.
  ,, Frankish, early, ii. 30.
  ,, French colours, ii. 3, 32.
  ,, Uri, shield of, ii. 11 *n*.
Hercules and the Nemean Lion, iii. 54.
Herod and the three Kings (Amiens Cathedral), iv. 50-51.
Herodotus on Egyptian influence in Greece, iii. 27.
Hilda, derivation of, ii. 48.
Hildebert, derivation of, ii. 48.
Hildebrandt, derivation of, ii. 48.
History, division of, into four periods of 500 years each, ii. 1.
  ,, how it is usually written, i. 17-19.

History, how it should be written, pref. iv.
,, popular, its effect on youthful minds, i. 19.
,, should record facts, not make reflections, iii. 26.
,, ,, ,, ,, ,, or suppositions, iii. 33 *n*.
Holy Land, iii. 14.
Honour, of son to father, iv. 17.
Hope, figure of, Amiens Cathedral, iv. 41.
Hosea, ,, ,, ,, iv. 43.
Huet, Alexander, and Amiens Cathedral choir, iv. 5 *n*.
Humanity, its essentials (love, sense, discipline), iv. 59.
Humility, no longer a virtue, iii. 4.
,, sculpture of, Amiens Cathedral, iv. 41.
Huns, the, in France, i. 14.

IDOLATRY and atheism, iv. 41.
,, figure of, Amiens Cathedral, iv. 41.
,, and symbolism, distinct, iv. 36.
Illyria, iii. 23.
Immortality, ii. 13.
India and England, iii. 16.
Indians, North American, ii. 48.
Infidelity, modern, i. 19; ii. 28; iii. 2.
Ingelow, Miss, quoted, "Songs of Seven," ii. 4.
Innocents, the Holy (Amiens Cathedral), iv. 51.
Inscription on tombs of Bishops Everard and Geoffroy, iv. 24, 26.
Inspiration of acts and words, not distinct, iii. 48.
,, of Scripture, modern views of, *ib.*
Invasion is not possession of a country, iii. 16.
Ireland and England, 1880, pref. i. ii.; iii. 6.
,, tribes of, in early Britain, iii. 24 *n*.
Isaiah, figure of, Amiens Cathedral, iv. 38, 42.
Italy, under the Ostrogoths, iii. 16.

JACOB'S pillow, iii. 26.
Jameson, Mrs., "Legendary Art" quoted, i. 23 *n.*, 28.
Jeremiah, figure of, Amiens Cathedral, iv. 38, 42.
Jerusalem, fall of, iii. 39.
Jews, the, and Assyria, iii. 18.
,, ,, return to Jerusalem, iii. 39.
,, ,, substitute usury for prophecy, iii. 19.

Joan of Arc, ii. 7, 55 ; iv. 7.
Joel, figure of, Amiens Cathedral, iv. 43.
Johnson, Dr., iv. 17 *n*.
Jonah, figure of, Amiens Cathedral, iv. 43.
Julian, the Emperor, rejects auguries, iii. 26 *n*.
,, ,, and Constantius, ii. 31 *n*.
,, ,, death of, 363 A.D., iii. 34, 36.
,, ,, defeats the Franks, 358 A.D., ii. 35.
,, ,, refortifies the Rhine against the Franks, ii. 28 *n*.
,, ,, and St. Martin, i. 24.
,, ,, victory of, at Strasbourg, ii. 35.
Justinian, a Dacian by birth, ii. 15 *n*.
,, means "upright," ii. 15 *n*.

KALTENBACHER, Mons., photographs of Amiens Cathedral, iv. 47.
Karr, Alphonse, his work and the author's sympathy with it, i. 36.
,, ,, his 'Grains de Bons Sens,' 'Bourdonnements,' i. 36.
Kempis, Thomas à, iii. 44.
Kingliness, ii. 43.
Kings, the three (Amiens Cathedral), iv. 50-51.
Knighthood, belted, meaning of, ii. 34.
Knowledge, true, is of virtue, pref. iv.

LAON Cathedral, legend of, and oxen, iv. 41 *n*.
Latin and English compared, iv. 24 seq.
Law, the force of, and government, iii. 15.
,, old and new forms of, ii. 43.
Lear, King, story of, reduced to its bare facts, i. 17-18.
Legends, true or not, immaterial, i. 23 seqq.; iii. 54.
,, modern contempt for, iv. 46.
,, rationalization of, its value, ii. 47 *n*.
Leopard, English heraldic, ii. 31.
Leucothea, ii. 3.
Liberté, Egalité, Fraternité, ii. 42.
Liberty, and activity, ii. 29.
,, and "franchise," ii. 27, 28 *n*.
Libya, iii. 13.
,, and Vandal invasion, iii. 16.

Lily on statue of David, Amiens Cathedral, iv. 32.
Limousins, i. 16.
Lion, under feet of Christ, Amiens Cathedral, iv. 34.
Literature and art, distinct mental actions, iii. 47.
    ,,   and the Bible, iii. 51.
    ,,   cheap (penny edition of Scott), iii. 7.
Louis, derivation of, ii. 48.
—— I., of France, ii. 40.
—— VIII., iv. 16.
        See ss. Louis.
Love, divine and human (Amiens Cathedral), iv. 41.
    ,, no humanity without it, iv. 59.
Luca della Robbia, iii. 46.
Luini, iii. 46.
Lune, the river, i. 3.
Lust (Amiens Cathedral), iv. 41.
Lydia, iii. 12.

MADONNA, figure of, Amiens Cathedral, iv. 7.
    ,,   porch to, ,,   ,,   iv. 28.
    ,,   three types of (Dolorosa, Reine, Nourrice), iv. 49.
    ,,   worship of, and its modern substitutes, iv. 48.
Malachi, figure of, Amiens Cathedral, iv. 43.
Man, races of, divided by climate, iii. 8.
Man's nature, iii. 1.
Manchester, iii. 3.
Map-drawing, iii. 7.
    ,, of English dominions (Sir E. Creasy), iii. 5 6.
    ,, of France, i. 12.
    ,, on Mercator's projection, iii. 6.
Marquise, village near Calais, i. 16.
Martin's, John, "Belshazzar's feast," iv. 42.
Martinmas, i. 29.
Martyrdom, the lessons of, iv. 53.
Martyrs, female, many not in calendar, ii. 7.
Meleager, ii. 11.
Memory, "Memoria technica," ii. 1.
Mercator, iii. 6.
Merovée, seizes Amiens, on death of Clodion, 447 A.D., i. 11, 34.
Micah, figure of, Amiens Cathedral, iv. 43.

Millennium, the, iii. 54.
Milman's History of Christianity, iii. 22, 26, 32.
,,   ,,   ,,   on Rome *temp.* S. Jerome, iii. 35.
Milton's "Paradise Lost," and the Bible, iii. 44.
,,   ,,   ,,   quoted, iv. 41.
Mind, disease of, noble and ignoble passion, iii. 29.
Mines, coal, Plimsoll on, ii. 42.
Missals, atheism represented as barefoot in, of 1100-1300, ii. 41.
Modernism, avarice and pride of, iv. 35. See s. Christianity, Commerce, England, History, Humility, Infidelity, Philosophy, Public Opinion, Science.
Mœsia, and the alphabet, iii. 22.
Monasteries of Italy, made barracks of, iii. 29 *n.*
Monasticism, its rise, iii. 26-28.
Monks, type of character of, iii. 29 ; iv. 56.
,,   orders of, the main, iii. 26.
Months, the, quatrefoils illustrative of (Amiens Cathedral), iv. 47.
Morality, natural to man, iv. 59.
,,   and religion, iv. 58.
More, Sir Thomas, execution of, ii. 43.
Morocco, extent of, iii. 13.
Moses, iii. 26.
,,   and Aaron, iv. 51.
,,   and the burning bush, iv. 51.
"Mysteries of Paris," ii. 5.

NAHUM, figure of, Amiens Cathedral, iv. 43 and *n.*
Names, Frankish, etymology of, ii. 48.
Nanterre, village of S. Genevieve, ii. 5, 8.
Nationality, depends on race and climate, not on rule, iii. 15-16.
Nemean Lion, iii. 53.
Netherlands, the, ii. 26.
Nineveh, the beasts in, iv. 43.
,,   the burden of, iv. 43.
Nitocris, ii. 6.
Nogent, Benedictine abbey of, ii. 49.
Nomad tribes of northern Europe, ii. 10.
Normans, rise of the, ii. 12.
Νοῦς, iv. 59 *n.*

OBADIAH, figure, of, Amiens Cathedral, iv. 43.
Obedience, figure of, Amiens Cathedral, iv. 41.
Odoacer, ends Roman Empire in Italy, i. 12 ; iii. 21.
Orcagna, iii. 46.
Origen, iii. 47.
Ostrogoths, ii. 12.
  ,,   defeat Clovis at Arles, ii. 47.
"Our Fathers have told us," aim, origin, and plan, pref. i.
    ,,   ,,   general plan of, App. iii.
    ,,   ,,   plan for notes to, i. 34.
Oxen, story of, and Laon Cathedral, iv. 41.
  ,, patience of, iv. 41.
Oxford, the "happy valley," iv. 6.

PALESTINE, iii. 14.
Palgrave, Sir F., on Arabia, iii. 17-18 and *n*.
    ,,   ,,   on the camel, iv. 41.
Papacy, origin of the, iii. 35 *n*.
Paris, church of St. Genevieve at, ii. 55.
  ,, the Isle of France, iv. 58.
  ,, the model of manners, iv. 58.
  ,, print-shops at, iv. 41.
Patience, figure of, Amiens Cathedral, iv. 41.
Peasant life of early Europe, ii. 13.
Perseverance, figure of, Amiens Cathedral, iv. 41.
Persia, the real power of the East, iii. 18.
Philip the Wise, of France, iv. 16-17.
Philistia, iii. 14.
Philosophy, modern, its manner of history, i. 19.
Phœnix, the, and chastity, iv. 41.
Photographs of Amiens Cathedral, iv. 41 *n*., 43 *n*., 201 ; App. ii.
"Pilgrim's Progress," i. 25.
Pillage of subjects, to punish kings, ii. 51.
Plimsoll, on coal mines, ii. 42.
Poets, the three Christian-heathen, iv. 20.
Poitiers, battle of, 508 A.D., Clovis and Alaric, i. 13, 34.
    ,,   ,,   and the walls of Angoulême, ii. 47 *n*.
    ,,   ,,   1356 A.D., Froissart on, ii. 33.
Polacks, the, ii. 12.
Politicians, their proper knowledge, pref. iv.

INDEX.   303

Politics, see s. England.
Posting days, Calais to Paris, i. 16.
Power, motive of desire for, iii. 33.
Praise, all great art, act, and thought is, pref. iv.
Prayer, George Chapman's last, iv. 20.
Pride, and avarice, iv. 35.
,,   faults and virtues of, iv. 24.
,,   infidelity of, and the cockatrice, iv. 33, 41.
Priestly ambition, iii. 33.
Probus, the Emperor, ii. 15 *n.*; iii. 21.
Prophets, figures of the, Amiens Cathedral, general view of, iv. 39.
   ,,   ,,   ,,   ,,   in detail, iv. 42-43.
Protestantism, and the study of the Bible, iii. 45.
   ,,   and popular histories, i. 18.
   ,,   and priestly ambition, iii. 33.
   ,,   and Roman Catholicism, iv. 57.
   ,,   views of S. Jerome, iii. 31.
Provence, early, i. 12, 14.
Providence, God's, and history, i. 19.
Psalms, the scope of the, iii. 50.
Public opinion, callousness of modern, ii. 42.
Purgatory, doctrine of, iv. 55 *n.*
Puritan malice, ii. 19.

QUAKER, preaching at Matlock, iii. 48 *n.*
Queen's Guards, in Ireland, 1880, pref. ii.

RACES of Europe, divided by climate, iii. 9. See s. Climate.
Rachel, the Syrian, iii. 14.
Railroads, modern, of Germany, iii. 4.
   ,,   travelling by, i. 1, 4.
Raphael's Madonnas, iv. 49.
Rebellion, figure of, Amiens Cathedral, iv. 41.
Religion, definition of true, iv. 60. And see s. Bible, Christianity, Inspiration, Protestantism.
   ,,   to desire the right, iii. 48.
   ,,   common idea that our own enemies are God's also, i. 21.
   ,,   and morality, iv. 58.
   ,,   natural, iv. 20.
   ,,   of Arabia, iii. 19.

Religion, of Egypt, iii. 13.
,,   Eastern and Western, Col. Butler on, i. 34-35.
Restoration, modern, iv. 27 *n.*
Rheims Cathedral, iv. 1.
,,   ,,   its traceries, iv. 11.
,,   Clovis crowned at, i. 13.
,,   ,,   enriches church of, ii. 49.
Rhine, the, refortified by Julian, ii. 28 *n.*, 31.
,,   ,,   tribes from Vistula to, ii. 10.
Right and left, in description of cathedrals, iv. 28.
Rivers, strength and straightness, iii. 10 *n.*
Robert, of Luzarches, builder of Amiens Cathedral, iv. 12.
Roman Catholics, half Wellington's army Irish, pref. iii.
,,   ,,   and Protestantism, iv. 57.
,,   ,,   servants, iii. 29.
,,   Emperors, five, from Dacia, ii. 15 *n.*
,,   ,,   as supreme Pontiffs, iii. 35.
Roman Empire, divisions of (Illyria, Italy, Gaul), iii. 21-22.
,,   ,,   Eastern and Western division, iii. 21.
,,   ,,   end of the, iii. 20-21.
,,   ,,   fall of, ii. 12.
,,   ,,   ,, and Julian and the augurs, iii. 26.
,,   ,,   its main foes, ii. 9.
,,   ,,   its true importance, iii. 20.
,,   ,,   a power, not a nation, iii. 19 *n.*
,,   ,,   power of, in France, ends, 481 A.D., i. 6-7, 12.
,,   ,,   ,, in Italy, ends, 476 A.D., i. 12.
Roman gate of Twins, at Amiens, i. 22.
" Romaunt of the Rose," quoted, ii. 28 *n.*
Rome, aspect of the city, *temp.* S. Jerome, iii 35.
,,   gives order to Europe, as Greece imagination, iii. 20.
,,   wild nations opposed to, ii. 9.
Romsey, i. 3.
Rose, on statue of David, Amiens Cathedral, iv. 32.
Rosin forest, ii. 20-21.
Royalties, taxes and, ii. 41.
Rozé, Père, on Amiens Cathedral, iv. 13, 24 *n.*, 43.

S. ACHEUL., near Amiens, iv. 45-46.
S. Agnes, character of, ii. 3.

S. Ambrogio, Verona, plain of, ii. 54.
S. Augustine, first converts of, i. 29.
    ,,   S. Jerome and, iii. 47.
    ,,   town of Hippo, iii. 13.
S. Benedict, born 481 A.D., ii. 3; iii. 26.
S. Clotilde, of France, ii. 48.
S. Cloud, etymology of, ii. 48.
S. Domice, iv. 44.
S. Elizabeth, iv. 50.
S. Elizabeth, of Marburg, ii. 21-23.
S. Firmin, his history, i. 6 seqq.; iv. 14, 45.
    ,,   beheaded and buried, i. 7.
    ,,   his Roman disciple, i. 8.
    ,,   his grave, i. 8 seqq.; iv. 46.
    ,,   and S. Martin, compared, i. 29.
    ,,   porch to, Amiens Cathedral, iv. 28, 44.
    ,,   sculpture of, Amiens Cathedral, i. 8.
St. Firmin, Confessor, iv. 44-46.
St. Fuscien, iv. 44.
S. Genevieve, actually existed, ii. 7.
    ,,   biographies of her, numerous, ii. 7.
    ,,   birth of, 421 A.D., ii. 3.
    ,,   birthplace of, Nanterre, ii. 5.
    ,,   character of, ii. 5-7.
    ,,   church to, at Paris, ii. 55.
    ,,   and Clovis and his father, ii. 55.
    ,,   conversion of, by S. Germain, ii. 5.
    ,,   a pure Gaul, ii. 8, 15.
    ,,   of what typical, ii. 3.
    ,,   peacefulness, ii. 6.
    ,,   quiet force, ii. 7.
    ,,   S. Phyllis, ii. 5.
S. Gentian, iv. 44.
S. Geoffroy, Bishop of Amiens, history of, iv. 44-45.
    ,,   ,,   ,,   tomb of (Amiens), iv, 24, 26.
S. Germain converts S. Genevieve, on his way to England, ii. 6.
S. Hilda (Whitby Cliff), ii. 48.
S. Honoré, iv. 44-45.
    ,,   porch to, Amiens Cathedral, iv. 7.
S. James, apostle of hope, iv. 41.

S. Jerome, his Bible, iii. 26, 36, 37-40.
,, gives the Bible to the West, ii. 47.
,, Galatians, commentary on Epistle to the, iii. 47.
,, character of, candour its basis, iii. 36.
,, childhood and early studies, iii. 34-35.
,, death of, at Bethlehem, iii. 40.
,, Hebrew, studied by, iii. 38.
,, not a mere hermit, iii. 31.
,, his lion, iii. 53.
,, Milman, Dean, on, iii. 32 seq.
,, Protestant view of, iii. 31.
,, Queen Sophia's letter to Vota on, iii. 47.
,, scholarship will not give up his, iii. 36.
,, style of writing shown, iii. 47.
S. John, the apostle of love, iv. 37.
,, his greatness, iv. 16.
S. Louis, religion under, i. 34.
S. Mark's, Venice, Baptistery of, and the virtues, iv. 36 *n*.
S. Martin, baptism and conversion of, i. 23.
,, character of, gentle and cheerful, i. 24, 29 seqq.
,, ,, patient, ii. 7.
,, ,, serene and sweet, i. 28.
,, cloak given to the beggar by, 332 A.D., i. 23.
,, Clovis and, i. 32.
,, Devil, answer to the, i. 28.
,, drinks to a beggar, i. 30.
,, fame of, universal (places called after), i. 29.
,, history of, how relevant to this book, i. 32.
,, 's Lane, London, i. 29.
,, and Julian, i. 24.
,, Tours, his abbey there, i. 33.
,, ,, and bishopric, i. 25, 31.
,, vision of, i. 23.
,, wine, the patron of, i. 29, 31.
S. *Nicholas, Journal de*, iv. 41 *n*.
S. Peter, Apostle of courage, iv. 37.
S. Quentin, iv. 44.
S. Remy crowns Clovis, i. 13.
,, preaches to Clovis, i. 20.
,, and the Soissons vase, ii. 41.

S. Sauve, iv. 14, 44.
S. Simeon, iv. 50.
S. Ulpha, i. 198; iv. 44, 46.
S. Victoric, iv. 44.
Salian, epithet of the French, ii. 30-31.
Salii, the, ii. 30.
Salique law, ii. 30.
Salisbury Cathedral, iv. 1.
"Salts," old and young, ii. 31.
Salvation, Protestant theory of, iii. 43.
Sands, English, i. 3.
Savage races, love of war in, ii. 48.
,, women, endurance a point of honour with, ii. 48.
Saxons, the, ii. 12.
,, religion of, i. 34-35.
Scandinavia, iii. 10.
,, becomes Norman, ii. 12.
Scepticism, modern, i. 19. See s. Infidelity.
Science, modern, its view of man, iii. 1.
Scotch crofters and England, iii. 6.
Scots, Picts and, iii. 24 *n*.
Scott, Sir Walter, his nomenclature deeply founded, ii. 18.
,, ,, novels of, "Antiquary" (Waldeck), ii. 18.
,, ,, ,, "Monastery," iii. 29 *n*.
,, ,, penny edition of, iii. 7.
Sculpture, of a Gothic cathedral, iv. 2.
,, no pathos in primary, iv. 19 *n*.
Scythia, tribes of, iii. 10, 17.
Semiramis, ii. 6.
Sense (νοῦς), essential to humanity, iv. 59.
Servants, Catholic, character of, iii. 29 *n*.
,, French, perfect, ii. 28.
Severn, the, i. 3.
Shakspeare's Imogen, ii. 3.
,, "King Lear," reduced to its bare facts, ii. 35.
,, "Winter's Tale"—"lilies of all kinds," iv. 32
Sheba, Queen of, and Solomon, Amiens sculptures, iv. 50-51.
Shield, the, of the Franks, i. 70; ii. 35. See s. Heraldry, Uri.
Shyness and frankness, ii. 28 and *n*.

Siberian wilderness, iii. 9, 10.
Sicambri, ii. 18, 27.
Sidney, Sir Philip, i. 23.
Sin, carnal, the most distinctly human, iv. 34.
  ,, deceit, its essence, ii. 44.
  ,, pardon of, doctrine of, iv. 55.
Slang, iv. 25.
  ,, Greek, iv. 59.
Smith's Dictionary, s. Gallia, ii. 9.
Soissons, battle of, 485 A.D., i. 10 n., 13, 34; ii. 49.
  ,, vase of, ii. 40 seq.
  ,, ,, and Clovis' revenge, ii. 43.
Solomon and Queen of Sheba (Amiens Cathedral), iv. 50-51.
Solway, the, i. 3.
Sons, honour of fathers by, iv. 17.
Spain, Theodoric in, ii. 53.
Spiritual world, the, iv. 59.
Staubbach, the, iv. 9.
Stone saw, not used in France, iv. 2 n.
Strigi, S. Jerome born at, iii. 34.
Suicide and heroism, iv. 41.
"Suisse Historique," quoted, ii. 49 n.
Sword, belted, meaning of, ii. 43.
  ,, manufacture, Amiens, iv. 43.
Syagrius defeated by Clovis, ii. 49.
  ,, dies, 486 A.D., ii. 49.
Syria, iii. 14.

TEMPERANCE, figure of, Amiens Cathedral, iv. 41.
Teutonic nations and Roman Empire, iii. 22.
Theodobert, the death of, ii. 11 n.
Thedoric, King of Ostrogoths, ii. 48.
  ,, defeats Franks at Arles, ii. 53.
  ,, power of, in Europe, ii. 53.
  ,, at Verona, ii. 54.
Thrace, iii. 23.
Thuringia, i. 10.
Tolbiac, battle of, i. 13, 34.
  ,, field of, ii. 54.
  ,, its real importance, ii. 52.

Tombs, bronze, Amiens Cathedral, iv. 23.
,, ,, only two left in France, iv. 23.
Tours, Archbishop of, on war, ii. 33.
,, S. Martin, bishop of, i. 25, 31.
Town, a modern, defined, iv. 3.
Tripoli, iii. 13.
Troy, iii. 12.
Trupin, Jean, and choir of Amiens Cathedral, iv. 5 *n*.
Truth, only, *can* be polished, ii. 16.
,, of French character, ii. 16.
Tunis, iii. 13.
Turner's "Loire side," i. 31.
Tyre, iii. 13.

ULPHILAS, Bible of, iii. 22.
Ulverstone, etymology of, iv. 46.
Uri, shield of, ii. 11 *n*.
Usury and the Church, i. 19.
,, and the Jews, iii. 19.
Utilitas, i. 11.

VALENS, his prefecture of the East, iii. 21.
Valentinian, and the division of the Empire, iii. 21.
Vandals, invasion of Libya by, iii. 16.
Venice, founded 421 A.D., i. 2.
Verona, Cathedral of, iv. 1.
,, battle of, Theodoric defeats Odoacer, 490 A.D., ii. 54
,, field of, from Fra Giocondo's bridge, ii. 54.
Vestal Virgins, iii. 26.
Violence, expression of, in sculptures of Amiens, iv. 43.
Viollet le Duc, quoted, iv. 1, 2, 11, 23 *n*., 36, 41 *n*., 49
Vine, on statue of David, Amiens Cathedral, iv. 32.
Virgil's influence on Dante, iii. 53.
Virgil quoted (Æneid vi. 27 seq.), iv. 18 19 *n*.
Virgin, the. See s. Madonna.
Virtue, to be known and recognized, pref. iv.
Virtues, of Apostles (Amiens Cathedral), iv. 37 seq.
,, Byzantine, rank of, iv. 36 *n*.
Visigoths, the, ii. 12.
,, ,, in France, i. 12, 14.
,, ,, at Poitiers, defeated by Clovis, i. 13.

U

Vistula, the, its importance, iii. 9, 10.
,, ,, tribes of, from Rhine to, ii. 10, 12
,, ,, ,, ,, Weser to, ii. 26.
Vobiscum," a "Pax, iv. 38 *n*.
Vota, the Jesuit, letter of Queen Sophia of Prussia to, on St. Jerome, iv. 47. (See Carlyle's "Frederick," Bk. I., cap. iv.)
Vulgate, Ps. xci. 13, "Inculcabis super leonem," iv. 34.

WALDECK, ii. 18.
Walter's houses, Germany, ii. 25.
Walton, Isaac, i. 2.
Wandle, the, i. 2.
War, savage love of, ii. 48.
Wartzburg, ii. 24.
Wellington, Duke of, on Roman Catholic valour, pref. iii.
Weser, the course of the, ii. 19, 26.
,, sources of the (Eder, Fulda, Werra), ii. 24.
,, tribes of the, up to Rhine and Vistula, ii. 26.
Whitby Cliff, ii. 48.
Wisdom, figure of, Amiens Cathedral, iv. 41.
Women, endurance a point of honour with savage, ii. 48.
,, respect for, by Franks and Goths, ii. 54.
Wood-carving of Picardy (Amiens Cathedral), iv. 5 seq.
Wool manufacture, Amiens. See s. Amiens.
Wordsworth quoted, "Filling more and more with crystal light," ii. 55.

YONGE, Miss, "History of Christian Names," Franks, ii. 27.
,, ,, ,, ,, ,, Ulpha, iv. 46.

ZACHARIAS, iv. 51.
Zechariah, figure of, Amiens Cathedral, iv. 43.
Zenobia, ii. 6.
Zephaniah, figure of, Amiens Cathedral, iv. 43.
Zodiac, signs of, sculptures, Amiens Cathedral, iv. 47.
Zulu War, the, ii. 43 ; iii. 6.

www.ingramcontent.com/pod-product-compliance
Lightning Source LLC
Chambersburg PA
CBHW021207230426
43667CB00006B/600